NML /AF

▶ **Refugees, Prisoners and Camps**

DOI: 10.1057/9781137502797.0001

Other Palgrave Pivot Titles

Emily F. Henderson: **Gender Pedagogy: Teaching, Learning and Tracing Gender in Higher Education**

Mihail Evans: **The Singular Politics of Derrida and Baudrillard**

Bryan Fanning and Andreas Hess: **Sociology in Ireland: A Short History**

Tom Watson (editor): **Latin American and Caribbean Perspectives on the Development of Public Relations: Other Voices**

Anshu Saxena Arora and Sabine Bacouël-Jentjens (editors): **Advertising Confluence: Transitioning the World of Marketing Communications into Social Movements**

Bruno Grancelli: **The Architecture of Russian Markets: Organizational Responses to Institutional Change**

Michael A. Smith, Kevin Anderson, Chapman Rackaway, and Alexis Gatson: **State Voting Laws in America: Voting Fraud, or Fraudulent Voters?**

Nicole Lindstrom: **The Politics of Europeanization and Post-Socialist Transformations**

Madhvi Gupta and Pushkar: **Democracy, Civil Society, and Health in India**

George Pattison: **Paul Tillich's Philosophical Theology: A Fifty-Year Reappraisal**

Alistair Cole and Ian Stafford: **Devolution and Governance: Wales between Capacity and Constraint**

Kevin Dixon and Tom Gibbons: **The Impact of the 2012 Olympic and Paralympic Games: Diminishing Contrasts, Increasing Varieties**

Felicity Kelliher and Leana Reinl: **Green Innovation and Future Technology: Engaging Regional SMEs in the Green Economy**

Brian M. Mazanec and Bradley A. Thayer: **Deterring Cyber Warfare: Bolstering Strategic Stability in Cyberspace**

Amy Barnes, Garrett Wallace Brown and Sophie Harman: **Global Politics of Health Reform in Africa: Performance, Participation, and Policy**

Densil A. Williams: **Competing against Multinationals in Emerging Markets: Case Studies of SMEs in the Manufacturing Sector**

Nicos Trimikliniotis, Dimitris Parsanoglou and Vassilis S. Tsianos: **Mobile Commons, Migrant Digitalities and the Right to the City**

Claire Westall and Michael Gardiner: **The Public on the Public: The British Public as Trust, Reflexivity and Political Foreclosure**

Federico Caprotti: **Eco-Cities and the Transition to Low Carbon Economies**

Emil Souleimanov and Huseyn Aliyev: **The Individual Disengagement of Avengers, Nationalists, and Jihadists: Why Ex-Militants Choose to Abandon Violence in the North Caucasus**

palgrave▶pivot

Refugees, Prisoners and Camps: A Functional Analysis of the Phenomenon of Encampment

Bjørn Møller

Professor, Department of Political Science, AAU-Copenhagen

Lecturer, Centre of African Studies, University of Copenhagen

palgrave
macmillan

DOI: 10.1057/9781137502797.0001

First published 2015 by
PALGRAVE MACMILLAN

Palgrave Macmillan in the UK is an imprint of Macmillan Publishers Limited, registered in England, company number 785998, of Houndmills, Basingstoke, Hampshire RG21 6XS.

Palgrave Macmillan in the US is a division of St Martin's Press LLC, 175 Fifth Avenue, New York, NY 10010.

Palgrave Macmillan is the global academic imprint of the above companies and has companies and representatives throughout the world.

Palgrave® and Macmillan® are registered trademarks in the United States, the United Kingdom, Europe and other countries.

ISBN: 978-1-137-50280-3 EPUB
ISBN: 978-1-137-50279-7 PDF
ISBN: 978-1-137-50278-0 Hardback

A catalogue record for this book is available from the British Library.

A catalog record for this book is available from the Library of Congress.

www.palgrave.com/pivot

DOI: 10.1057/9781137502797

Contents

DOI: 10.1057/9781137502797.0001

DOI: 10.1057/9781137502797.0001

List of Illustrations

Figure

Tables

Preface

'Camp' is a word with many meanings and very different connotations, ranging from the very positive (e.g., the summer camps to which many parents send their kids) to the extremely negative as in the German concentration camps such as Auschwitz.

This may be due to coincidence, as when the word 'tit' both refers to a family of birds (with the Latin name *paridae*), to a special part of the female anatomy (slang for breast), and to the opposite of 'tat' as in the 'tit-for-tat' (meaning 'equivalent retaliation') which seems to have no independent meaning. However, it is also conceivable that there is actually a group of phenomena which have enough in common for them to be conceptualised as a genus with various species. It may also be that there may be a kind of 'blueprint' of camps of which the various actually existing camps are different versions, either in the 'form' or 'idea' as envisioned by Plato and his followers,[1] or what Max Weber (in more or less the same vein) called an 'ideal-type' of camp to which actual camps may be approximations. According to the German sociologist such an ideal-type does not exist in reality, but it is a mere mental construct:

> An ideal type is formed by the one-sided accentuation of one or more points of view and by the synthesis of a great many diffuse, discrete, more or less present and occasionally absent concrete individual phenomena, which are arranged according to those one-sidedly emphasized viewpoints into a unified analytical construct. (*Gedankenbild*)[2]

DOI: 10.1057/9781137502797.0003

One of the most wide-spread forms of contemporary camps is the refugee camps typically springing up around countries embroiled in armed conflict, or indeed within the very same countries where they host so-called IDPs (internally displaced persons). Either they are established by the fleeing people themselves as a means of protection by numbers and enfencement or, more often and certainly attracting more attention, they are established by various humanitarian organisations as a convenient setup for the provision of aid to endangered and destitute civilians – but such camps may also serve almost diametrically opposite ends, that is, serve as base areas for armed groups attacking their antagonists, perhaps including civilians outside the confines of the camp.

Not only does this ambivalence pertain to other categories of camps serving not just one purpose but occasionally also being used for exactly opposite end, but it may also apply to the ends or functions themselves, as when, for instance, one can achieve the same objectives by locking people in or out. These complexities almost invite some kind of 'dialectical' approach in the simple sense of seeking to understand a phenomenon by also looking at its opposite. Not only because the author is a historian by training, but also because he agrees with Kenneth Boulding's saying that 'Things are the way they are because they got that way' (occasionally with the elaboration 'have not always been that way, need not always be that way'),[3] he finds it important (or at the very least enlightening) to also look at phenomena such as camps in a historical and evolutionary perspective.

We thus end up with quite a tall order, that is, to analyse different categories of camps as well as their (more or less complete) functional equivalents and opposites and doing so in a historical perspective. Needless to say, this could not possibly be done in a work with the modest size of the present monograph, but would require a multi-volume work, ideally authored by renowned specialists in the different fields and disciplines. The present work has a much more limited ambition, that is, to provide an overview of the field and suggest new angles of analysis of various phenomena.

It commences with a brief and broad overview of the field, that is, the various phenomena that are usually referred to as camps, selecting certain categories for further analysis and *ipso facto* de-selecting others which will be omitted from analysis. It also presents an overview of the various academic disciplines that would seem to be in a position to illuminate various aspects of these phenomena, and it proceeds to outline some

DOI: 10.1057/9781137502797.0003

theoretical approaches to the study of camps, not least the foucauldian theory (if so it is) on 'heterotopias', understood as spaces of exception.

Then come lengthier outlines of some of the main camp categories in more or less random order: Prison camps and other penal institutions and facilities as well as their functional equivalents; concentration camps and the special category of extermination camps; prisoners-of-war camps and refugee and IDP camps – the latter also analysed as an important element in a broader refugee (or 'forced displacement') regime. These chapters are more empirical and historical than the others, but also arranged according to the same functionalist and dialectical principles – but the depth into which they go also reflects the author's main interests as well as the depth of his expertise. The refugee camps and equivalents thus receive most attention, reflecting the fact that the author teaches refugee studies at the University of Aalborg and is also involved in refugee matters as a member of the Refugee Appeals Board in his native Denmark. The chapter on concentration camps draws on quite extensive research on genocide, primarily undertaken for a much lengthier work on genocides, war crimes, crimes against humanity and the so-called responsibility to protect which the author is also striving to complete. The chapters on prisoner-of-war camps as well as the conflict-related sections of the refugee camps chapter are to a large extent based on the author's involvement in conflict studies for nearly 30 years, whereas the chapter on prison and other penal camps is related to a much more recent involvement in policing studies.

Notes

1   Plato (1892) 'Phaedo,' in B. Jowett (ed.) From Plato to (ed.) *The Dialogues of Plato in Five Volumes*. 3rd ed. (Oxford: Oxford University Press) II, 195–266, especially 220–222; idem 'The Republic,' ibid., III, 1–338, especially Book VII, 214–217.

2   M. Weber (1963) 'Objectivity in Social Science and Social Policy,' in M. Natanson (ed.) From Weber to (ed.) *Philosophy of the Social Sciences* (New York: Random House), 355–418, quoted on 498; idem (1981) 'Some Categories of Interpretive Sociology' (1913), in *Sociological Quarterly*, 22:2, 145–150.

3   See R. Lewontin and R. Levins 'A Program for Biology,' in idem and idem (eds.) From See to (eds) *Biology under the Influence: Dialectical Essays on Ecology, Agriculture and Health* (New York: Monthly Review Press), 81–86, quote from 85.

DOI: 10.1057/9781137502797.0003

List of Abbreviations

ADFL	Alliance des Forces Démocratiques pour la Libération du Congo-Zaïre (Alliance of Democratic Forces for the Liberation of Congo-Zaïre)
AliR	Armée pour la libération de Rwanda (Army for the Liberation of Rwanda)
ANC	African National Congress
AU	African Union
CCTV	Closed-Circuit Television
DPRK	Democratic People's Republic of Korea
ECHR	European Convention on Human Rights
EctHR	European Court of Human Rights
EPLF/A	Eritrean People's Liberation Front/Army
FDLR	*Forces démocratiques de libération du Rwanda* (Democratic Forces for the Liberation of Rwanda)
FLN	Front de Libération Nationale (National Liberation Front)
FRELIMO	Frente de Libertação de Moçambique (Front for the Liberation of Mozambique)
FRONTEX	European Agency for the Management of Operational Cooperation at the External Borders of the Member States of the European Union
GULAG	Glavnoe Upravlenie Lagerei
ICRC	International Committee of the Red Cross
IDMC	Internal Displacement Monitoring Centre
IDP	Internally Displaced Person
IHL	International Humanitarian Law

IRO	International Refugees Organization
LGBT	Lesbians, Gays, Bisexuals, and Transgender persons
LURD	Liberians United for Reconciliation and Democracy
MPLA	Movimento Popular de Libertação de Angola (Popular Liberation Movement of Angola)
NGOs	Non-Governmental Organisations
NKVD	Narodnyy Komissariat Vnutrennikh Del (People's Commissariat for Internal Affairs)
NRA	National Resistance Army
OAU	Organisation for African Unity
OLF	Operation Lifeline Sudan
PFLP	Popular Front for the Liberation of Palestine
PLO	Palestinian Liberation Organisation
PMC	Private Military Companies
POW	Prisoners-of-War
RCD	Rassemblement Congolais pour la Démocratie (Congolese Gathering for Democracy)
RENAMO	Resistência Nacional Moçambicana (Mozambican National Resistance)
RPF/A	Rwandan Patriotic Front/Army
SADC	Southern African Development Community
SPLM/A	Sudan People's Liberation Movement/Army
TPLF/A	Tigrayan People's Liberation Front/Army
UN	United Nations
UNHCR	United Nations' High Commissioner for Refugees
UNITA	União Nacional para a Independência Total de Angola (National Union for the Total Independence of Angola)
UNRWA	United Nations Relief and Works Agency for the Palestine Refugees in the Middle East
USSR	Union of Socialist Soviet Republics
WWII	World War II

DOI: 10.1057/9781137502797.0004

1
Introduction: Methods, Concepts and Theories

Abstract: *The introduction provides an overview of the subsequent analysis and a tentative classification of different types of camps, and an identification of the contributions of various academic disciplines to an understanding of camps. It also offers an explanation of the methodology, which is primarily functionalist, focusing on the functions of encampment, but also historical and dialectical in the sense of looking throughout at functional equivalents of encampment. It also introduces the theoretical concept of heteronomy, drawn from Michel Foucault.*

Keywords: asylum; camps; concentration camps; Foucault; ghettos; Gulag; heteronomy; prisoners-of-war camps; prisons; refugee camps; refugees; training camps

Møller, Bjørn. *Refugees, Prisoners and Camps: A Functional Analysis of the Phenomenon of Encampment.* Basingstoke: Palgrave Macmillan, 2015. DOI: 10.1057/9781137502797.0005.

In the following chapters 'camps' will be used in a rather broad sense as places of separation, segregation or confinement of people which are usually, but not necessarily, marked off with a fence or an equivalent thereof. They are treated as what Michel Foucault called 'heterotopias,' that is, 'places outside of all places' or 'outsides inside' and thus as exceptions.

1.1   History, functionalism and dialectics

The primary aim of this short monograph is to provide a functional analysis of camps, wherefore it distinguishes between various categories of camps according to the functions they are supposed to perform. In most cases the origins and historical development of each category are briefly outlined.

The analysis is also partly 'dialectical,' albeit admittedly in a rather loose sense, perhaps more akin to Immanuel Kant's 'antinomies' than to G.W.F. Hegel's 'thesis-antithesis-synthesis' mode of thinking.[1] Having identified camps as performing a (set of) function(s), it then proceeds to 'represent, contest, and invert' (in the words of Foucault, *vide infra*) these functions by identifying functional equivalents of camps, some of which may also be 'places' or 'spaces,' whereas others are not. A good example, to which we shall return in Chapter 2, is Jeremy Bentham's famous blueprint of a prison known as the 'Panopticon' intended for correctional (as opposed to punitive) purposes. This has given rise to various other forms of surveillance, often lumped together as forms of 'panopticism,' which may take material form, for example, in the form of wiretapping and closed-circuit-TV surveillance, but the supposedly positive consequences of which may also be achieved by, for instance, certain religious belief sets. Whereas camps are thus spaces, their functional equivalents need not be.

However much we may like to extend the definition of camps, it would be unwise to go too far. For the concept to retain its analytical utility, camps must remain exceptions. We may well understand what Bob Dylan meant when he sang that 'Sometimes I think this whole world is one big prison yard/Some of us are prisoners, some of us are guards,'[2] just as we probably understand what is meant by allegations along the lines of 'North Korea is one large prison camp.' The gist of, and the intention behind, such formulations is surely laudable, but they erode the significant differences between those unfortunate North Koreans who are in

DOI: 10.1057/9781137502797.0005

fact incarcerated and the majority who are not. Even somewhat more accurate comparisons of territories such as the Gaza Strip with prisons are only really useful if used for a comparison of the residents of Gaza with the rest of the Palestinian nation, on the West Bank or in a diaspora situation (*vide infra*).[3]

As 'exceptional spaces' or, as Giorgio Agamben puts it, 'spaces (or states) of exception,'[4] camps are almost emblematic, no matter what kind of camp we are talking about: Prison camps, concentration camps, labour and death camps, prisoners-of-war camps, guerrilla or terrorist training camps, strategic hamlets or refugee or IDP (internally displaced person) camps, to all of which some space is devoted in the following.

1.2　Camps and academic discipline(s)

Just as camps and similar types of confinement, according to Foucault and others, play quite a central role in disciplining societies, discipline(s) also play a role in understanding the phenomenon/a of the camp, as a camp may look quite differently from the academic vantage points of, for instance, architecture, law, political science or anthropology. The study of camps thus almost cries out for multidisciplinary studies, even when approached from the present article's historical-functional-line up dialectical angle, which simply opens up for a wealth of interesting research avenues.

▶ History is obviously indispensable for tracing the genealogy of contemporary camps, but it would be unwise to narrow this down to traditional (written) history based on archival studies and the reading of autobiographies and memoirs (e.g., of concentration camp commanders, staff and inmates), as there is also a role for oral history, as far as the not-too-distant past is concerned.

▶ Archaeology may also prove relevant, especially for the study of the more distant past, and works have indeed been published with the ambition of founding so exotic sub-disciplines as the 'archaeology of internment' or even 'prisoner-of-war archaeology,' specialising in excavations at former prisoners-of-war camps.[5]

▶ Political science as well as political philosophy are relevant as vantage points for studying the links between various forms of camps and their functional equivalents and governmentality in the sense of Foucault. Might societies dispense with prisons in which to incarcerate habitual offenders, for instance, and which functional equivalents might be relevant? Would all-encompassing and around-the-clock surveillance help reduce crime and promote order, and what implications might this have for human rights, including the right to privacy?[6]

▶ Law, both international and national, is similarly relevant as this is (at least in most cases) the preferred instrument for deciding who should be incarcerated, on what grounds and under which conditions.

▶ Criminology and its sub-discipline of penology are interested in, among other things, for example, the pros and cons of punishment (today mainly in the form of imprisonment) v. correction; and in the consequences the constant 'gaze' which Benthamian panoptic spaces or arrangements may have on behaviour,[7] as well as on, for instance, the crime rates in modern 'ghettos' and what might be done about them.

▶ Economics has, for instance, proved relevant for the analysis of labour camps, such as those of the Soviet Gulag and some of the Nazi concentration camps, as business ventures, as well as for analysing the pros and cons of prison privatisation (*vide infra*).

▶ Architecture and urban planning are obvious disciplinary vantage points for studying the spatiality of camps[8] as well as camp-like features of special quarters of cities such as ghettos and 'gated communities' (*vide infra*).

▶ Sociology is obviously indispensable for uncovering and understanding the societal roles played by the various categories of camps as well as for analysing the internal social structures of the camps, as already argued by Hannah Arendt in 1950:

> [T]he institution of concentration and extermination camps, that is the social conditions within them as well their function in the larger terror apparatus to totalitarian regimes, may very likely become that unexpected phenomenon, that stumbling-block on the road toward the proper understanding of contemporary politics and society which must cause social scientists and historical scholars to reconsider their hitherto unquestioned fundamental preconceptions regarding the course of the world and human behavior.[9]

▶ Anthropology typically studies local communities from a bottom-up perspective, a methodology that allows for understanding the effects that camps and their equivalents have on community structures and the like, as we shall see in the section on refugee and IDP camps.

DOI: 10.1057/9781137502797.0005

▶ Psychology and social psychology may help analysing the special psychopathologies which are common to prisons, with the Zimbardo or Stanford prison experiment as the most dramatic case, where the experiment had to be terminated prematurely because of the extreme risks it turned out to constitute for the participants.[10]

1.3   Heterotopias: 'Outsides Inside'

As places of segregation, camps might be viewed as what Foucault called 'other spaces' or 'heterotopias,' that is,

> [R]eal places – places that do exist and that are formed in the very founding of society – which are something like counter-sites, a kind of effectively enacted utopia in which the real sites, all the other real sites that can be found within the culture, are simultaneously represented, contested, and inverted. Places of this kind are outside of all places, even though it may be possible to indicate their location in reality. Because these places are absolutely different from all the sites that they reflect and speak about, I shall call them, by way of contrast to utopias, heterotopias.[11]

This term has been used about as different phenomena as harems, gay nude beaches or university campuses,[12] but one might also mention other examples of 'outsides inside' societies where special rules apply. In some cases the special rules are *expressis verbis* formulated in laws and other authoritative regulations such as the following, the specificities for each of which may vary considerably, both over time and between countries, as it is all up for continuous negotiation.

▶ Spaces and places covered by diplomatic immunity cover not only embassies and their grounds, but also cars with diplomatic number-plates, diplomatic bags and, indeed, the very body of diplomats.[13] A person with a diplomatic passport suspected of having swallowed a condom filled with cocaine cannot, for instance, be subjected to a rectal search. In cases of abuse of this legal immunity, diplomats may thus be seen as 'privileged outlaws' and their abodes as extra-legal places.[14]

▶ The transit halls of airports where one is neither inside a country nor outside of it, which is also the case of various free ports, albeit mainly as the locus of goods rather than persons.[15] The case of the whistle-blower Edward Snowden in 2013 aptly illustrated the numerous unsettled issues in this respect – as did the film *The Terminal* from 2004, featuring Tom Hanks stranded at the J.F. Kennedy airport,[16] where he finds himself almost as shipwrecked and cast away as the same actor did in the leading role in the film *Cast Away* from 2000, a modern-day version of Daniel Defoe's *Robinson Crusoe*. The film *The Terminal* was (with lots of poetic licence) based on the real-life story of an Iranian refugee, Mehran Karimi Nasseri (aka 'Sir Alfred Mehran'), whose sojourn at the Charles De Gaulle airport lasted from 1988 to 2006 (*sic!*).[17]

▸ Ships are, according to Foucault, 'heterotopias par excellence.'[18] This is, for instance, the case when a ship belonging to a company from one state visits a harbour of another country where it enjoys a certain extraterritorial status.[19] The matter is further complicated if it flies a 'flag of convenience' because it has been registered in, for instance, Panama or Liberia or another 'open registry' state.[20] We shall return to this in the section about 'boat people.'

▸ Army barracks as well as military personnel are usually covered by military law and court martial jurisdiction rather than the 'law of the land' and patrolled by military police rather than the ordinary police force.[21]

▸ In hospitals the highest authorities are usually the doctors who can, at least under certain circumstances, deny the police access to their premises or at least their patients.[22]

▸ What is sometimes referred to as 'mass private property' may also constitute heterotopias, where tricky jurisdictional issues may pop up. This is, for instance, the case of shopping malls which are privately owned, but with free access for the public and often patrolled by private security companies;[23] or (at least in some countries) woods and beaches that are privately owned, but to which the proprietors are nevertheless obliged to allow public access.[24]

In olden days, church premises also constituted heterotopias where persons could seek refuge from the secular state authorities, as Esmeralda was granted when she was saved from the police by the hunchback Quasimodo and brought into the Notre Dame cathedral in the famous novel, *Notre Dame de Paris* by Victor Hugo:

> Meanwhile, after several moments of triumph, Quasimodo had plunged abruptly into the church with his burden. The populace, fond of all prowess,

DOI: 10.1057/9781137502797.0005

sought him with their eyes, beneath the gloomy nave, regretting that he had so speedily disappeared from their acclamations. All at once, he was seen to re-appear at one of the extremities of the gallery of the kings of France; he traversed it, running like a madman, raising his conquest high in his arms and shouting: 'Sanctuary!' The crowd broke forth into fresh applause. The gallery passed, he plunged once more into the interior of the church. A moment later, he re-appeared upon the upper platform, with the gypsy still in his arms, still running madly, still crying, 'Sanctuary!' and the throng applauded. Finally, he made his appearance for the third time upon the summit of the tower where hung the great bell; from that point he seemed to be showing to the entire city the girl whom he had saved, and his voice of thunder, that voice which was so rarely heard, and which he never heard himself, repeated thrice with frenzy, even to the clouds: 'Sanctuary! Sanctuary! Sanctuary!'

As far as the salvaged Esmeralda was concerned, 'She was outside the pale of society, outside the pale of life, but she had a vague feeling that it might not be impossible to return to it.'[25] At least she survived until betrayed by the sinister and devious arch-deacon Frollo.

One could also make a case for seeing 'Limbo' as a heterotopia of the afterlife according to, at least until quite recently, mainstream Catholic theology.[26] This was a rather dull 'place' for the non-baptised adults or infants who had committed no sins which should be punished in Hell or which would require redemption through a temporary sojourn in the Purgatory, but who were nevertheless, *qua* non-baptised, not eligible for going 'upstairs' into Paradise. However, in 2007 an International Theological Commission appointed by Pope John Paul II revisited the doctrine and found its status to be more dubious than previously assumed, a view that was subsequently endorsed by an '*imprimatur*' by the new pope, Benedict XVI.[27]

Besides the heterotopias formally constituted as such modern cities also contain socially constructed 'other spaces,' which are de facto reserved for special groups of people (usually held to be inferior by the rest of society) and where others enter at their own peril as in Dante's *Inferno*: '*Lasciate ogni esperanza, voi ch'entrate*' ('Leave all hope behind, thou who enters here').[28] Some places/spaces may be safe to visit at some times, but not for permanent residence, as is the case of Chinatowns around the world,[29] representing a kind of ghettos, to which we shall return in due course. The same could be said about the 'gated communities' found around the world, where the affluent few are protected from the less fortunate majority.[30] A case could surely also be made for seeing Europe

DOI: 10.1057/9781137502797.0005

as a large-scale gated community (viz. the term 'Fortress Europe')[31] where the rich EU member states are struggling to prevent refugees and illegal migrants (from Africa and the Middle East) from entering EU/Schengen territory where they would be able to apply for asylum. We shall return at some length to this issue in the chapter on refugee camps, also touching on Europe's *antechambers* such as the Italian island of Lampedusa and miscellaneous transit facilities.[32]

Notes

1   P.L. van den Berghe (1963) 'Dialectic and Functionalism: Toward a Theoretical Synthesis,' *American Sociological Review*, 28:5, 695–705; R.A. Ball (1979) 'The Dialectical Method: Its Application to Social Theory,' *Social Forces*, 57:3, 785–798. Kant's 'antinomies of pure reason' are described in I. Kant (1922) *Critique of Pure Reason*. 2nd ed. (London: Macmillan), 408–425. For a reminder that Hegel never explicitly used the thesis-antithesis-synthesis formula see G.E. Mueller (1958) 'The Hegel Legend of "Thesis-Antithesis-Synthesis",' *Journal of the History of Ideas*, 19:3, 411–414.

2   Quoted in J. Rodnitzky (1988) 'Also Born in the USA: Bob Dylan's Outlaw Heroes and the Real Bob Dylan,' *Popular Music and Society*, 12:2, 37–43.

3   Y. Lein (2005) *One Big Prison: Freedom of Movement to and from the Gaza Strip on the Eve of the Disengagement Plan* (Jerusalem: B'Tselem, at www.hamoked. org/items/12800_eng.pdf).

4   G. Agamben (2005) *State of Exception* (Chicago, IL: University of Chicago Press). See also C. Minca (2007) 'Agamben's Geographies of Modernity,' *Political Geography*, 26:1, 78–97; T. Basaran (2008) 'Security, Law, Borders: Spaces of Exclusion,' *International Political Sociology*, 2:4, 339–354; K. Schlosser (2008) 'Bio-Political Geographies,' *Geography Compass*, 2:5, 1621–1634.

5   G. Moshenka and A. Myers (2011) 'An Introduction to Archaeologies of Internment,' in A. Myers and G. Moshenka (eds.) *Archaeologies of Internment* (New York: Springer), 1–20; H. Mytum and G. Carr (2013) 'Prisoner of War Archaeology,' in idem (eds.) *Prisoners of War: Archaeology, Memory, and Heritage of 19th- and 20th-Century Mass Internment* (New York: Springer), 3–19; Harold Mytum, 'Prisoner of War Archaeology in an Interdisciplinary Context,' ibid., 321–332.

6   M. Foucault (1991) *Discipline and Punish: The Birth of the Prison* (London: Penguin); idem (2001) *Madness and Civilization: A History of Insanity in the Age of Reason* (London: Routledge), 35–60, 229–264.

7   J. Bentham (1838) 'Panopticon or, The Inspection House,' in *The Works of Jeremy Bentham*, IV (Edinburgh: William Tait), 37–175. See also N. Morris

and D.J. Rothman, eds. (1998) *The Oxford History of the Prison: The Practice of Punishment in Western Society* (Oxford: Oxford University Press).

8   A. Ramadan (2013) 'Spacialising the Refugee Camp,' *Transactions of the Institute of British Geographers*, 38:1, 65–77.

9   H. Arendt (1950) 'Social Science Techniques and the Study of the Concentration Camp,' *Jewish Social Studies*, 12:1, 49–64.

10 C. Haney, C. Banks and P. Zimbardo (1973). 'Interpersonal Dynamics in a Simulated Prison,' *International Journal of Criminology and Penology*, 1:1, 69–97; A. Jones (2011) *Genocide: A Comprehensive Introduction*. 2nd ed. (London: Routledge), 400–402.

11 M. Foucault (2002) *The Order of Things: An Archaeology of the Human Sciences* (London: Routledge), xix; M. Foucault and J. Miskowiec (1986) 'Of Other Spaces,' *Diacritics*, 16:1, 22–27, quote from p. 24. See also F. Boedeltje (2012) 'The Other Spaces of Europe: Seeing European Geopolitics through the Disturbing Eye of Foucault's Heterotopias,' *Geopolitics*, 17:1, 1–24; I. Sudradjat (2012) 'Foucault, the Other Spaces, and Human Behaviour,' *Procedia*, 36, 28–34; P. Johnson (2006) 'Unravelling Foucault's 'Different Spaces',' *History of the Human Sciences*, 19:4, 75–90; R.J. Topinka (2010) 'Foucault, Borges, Heterotopia: Producing Knowledge in Other Spaces,' *Foucault Studies*, 9, 54–70; H. Urbach (1998) 'Writing Architectural Heterotopia,' *Journal of Architecture*, 3:4, 347–354. See also the website www.heterotopiastudies.com/.

12 E.E. Akşit (2011) 'Harem Education and Heterotopic Imagination,' *Gender and Education*, 23:3, 299–311; K. Andriotis (2010) 'Heterotopic Erotic Oases: The Public Nude Beach Experience,' *Annals of Tourism Research*, 37:4, 1076–1096.

13 L.S. Frey and M.L. Frey (1999) *The History of Diplomatic Immunity* (Columbus, OH: Ohio State University Press).

14 M.B. McDonough (1997) 'Privileged Outlaws: Diplomats, Crime and Immunity,' *Suffolk Transnational Law Review*, 20:2, 475–500.

15 B. Ekeberg (2003) 'Life in Transit: A Global Condition,' *Topia*, 9, 83–96; K.E. Bite (2010) 'Staff Access Control at Airports,' *Transportation Engineering*, 38:1, 9–12.

16 R. Abeyratne (2014) 'Extradition and the Airport Transit Lounge: The Snowden Case,' *Journal of Transportation Security*, 7:1, 17–26.

17 H. Knox et al. (2007) 'Rites of Passage: Organization as an Excess of Flows,' *Scandinavian Journal of Management*, 23:3, 265–284; S.A. Hakim (2011) 'Destinations,' *Intervention*, 13:2, 299–317; J-B. Frétigny (2013) 'La frontière á l'épreuve des mobilités aériennes: Étude de l'aéroport de Paris Charles de Gaulle,' *Annales de Géographie*, 690, 151–174.

18 Foucault and Miskowiec, 'Of Other Spaces,' (n. 14), 27.

19 T.L. McDorman (2000) 'Regional Port State Control Agreements: Some Issues of International Law,' *Ocean and Coastal Law Journal*, 5:2, 207–226;

E.J. Molenaar (2007) 'Port State Jurisdiction: Towards Comprehensive, Mandatory and Global Coverage,' *Ocean Development and International Law*, 38:1–2, 225–257.

20   H.E. Anderson (1996) 'The Nationality of Ships and Flags of Convenience: Economics, Politics, and Alternatives,' *Tulane Maritime Law Journal*, 21:1, 139–170; J.E. Vorbach (2001) 'The Vital Role of Non-Flag State Actors in the Pursuit of Safer Shipping,' *Ocean Development and International Law*, 32:1, 27–42.

21   D.A. Schlueter (1980) 'The Court-Martial: An Historical Survey,' *Military Law Review*, 87:1, 129–166; J.W. Bishop Jr. (1964) 'Court-Martial Jurisdiction over Military-Civilian Hybrids: Retired Regulars, Reservists, and Discharged Prisoners,' *University of Pennsylvania Law Review*, 112: 3, 317–377.

22   A. Rogers (1993) 'Police and Psychiatrists: A Case of Professional Dominance,' *Social Policy and Administration*, 27:1, 33–44. On hospitals as heterotopias see A. Street and S. Coleman (2012) 'Introduction: Real and Imagined Spaces,' *Space and Culture*, 15:1, 4–17.

23   M. Kempa, P. Stenning and J. Wood (2004) 'Policing Communal Spaces: A Reconfiguration of the 'Mass Private Property' Hypothesis,' *British Journal of Criminology*, 44:4, 562–581; T. Jones and T. Newburn (1999) 'Urban Change and Policing: Mass Private Property Reconsidered,' *European Journal of Criminal Policy and Research*, 7:2, 225–244; M. Button (2003) 'Private Security and the Policing of Quasi-Public Space,' *International Journal of the Sociology of Law*, 31:3, 227–237.

24   C. Shearing and J. Wood (2003) 'Nodal Governance, Democracy, and the New 'Denizens',' *Journal of Law and Society*, 30:3, 400–419; E. Ostrom and C. Hess (2010) 'Private and Common Property Rights,' in B. Bouckaert (ed.) *Property Law and Economics* (Cheltenham: Edward Elgar), 53–106.

25   V. Hugo: *Notre Dame de Paris*, end of Book VIII and Book IX.4. English translation by I.F. Hapgood, at www.gutenberg.org/files/2610/2610-h/2610-h. htm.

26   G. D'Costa (2009) 'The Descent into Hell as a Solution to the Fate of Unevangelized Non-Christians: Balthasar's Hell, the Limbo of the Fathers and Purgatory,' *International Journal of Systematic Theology*, 11:2, 146–171.

27   International Theological Commission (2007) *The Hope of Salvation for Infants Who Die without Being Baptized* (Vatican, at www.vatican.va/ roman_curia/congregations/cfaith/cti_documents/rc_con_cfaith_ doc_ 20070419_un-baptised-infants_en.html). See also J. Thavis (2007) 'Vatican Commission: Limbo Reflects 'Restrictive View of Salvation',' *Catholic News Service*, 20 April 2007, at www.catholicnews.com/data/stories/ cns/0702216. htm.

28   'Leave all hope behind, thou who enters here.' See D. Alighieri, *Inferno*, III: 9, at www.divinecomedy.org/ divine_comedy.html.

DOI: 10.1057/9781137502797.0005

29 S.S.L. Bidlingmaier (2010) 'Spaces of Alterity and Temporal Permanence: The Case of San Francisco's and New York's Chinatowns,' in O. Kaltmeier (ed.) *Selling EthniCity: Urban Cultural Politics in the Americas* (Farnham, Surrey: Ashgate), 275–286; J. Lou (2007) 'Revitalizing Chinatown Into a Heterotopia: A Geosemiotic Analysis of Shop Signs in Washington D.C.'s Chinatown,' *Space and Culture*, 10: 2, 170–194.

30 D. Hook and M. Vrdoljak (2002) 'Gated Communities, Heteropia and a 'Rights' of Privilege: A 'Heterotopology' of the South African Security Park,' *Geoforum*, 33:2, 195–219.

31 M. Karskens (2008) 'The Political Frontiers of Europe as a Civil Society: J. Habermas' Rejection of a European *Volk* and M. Foucault's Balance of Power as Protections against European Nation-State,' *Limes*, 1:2, 186–198.

32 J. Pugliese (2009) 'Crisis Heterotopias and Border Zones of the Dead,' *Continuum*, 23:5, 663–679. See also the account by D. Fassin of the French detention centre or transit camp Sangatte in the chapter on 'Ambivalent Hospitality. Governing the Unwanted,' in idem (2012) *Humanitarian Reason: A Moral History of the Present* (Berkeley, CA: University of California Press), 133–157.

DOI: 10.1057/9781137502797.0005

2
Punitive and/or Preventative Confinement

Abstract: *Chapter 2 surveys the most common functions of prisons, that is, punishment, deterrence (both general and specific) and correction of criminals, as well as that of keeping them 'out of circulation.' As the latter often leads to prison overcrowding as well as rising costs, countries are experimenting with prison privatisation. It may even be possible to make incarceration profitable, by combining it with forced labour. This was part of the rationale of the huge Soviet Gulag camp system, but it failed regarding profitability. The chapter also looks at the phenomenon of panopticism as an alternative form of crime prevention as well as its functional equivalents. The chapter also covers the alternative way of separating deviants from the rest of society through deportation.*

Keywords: Bentham; correction; Gulag; incarceration; panopticism; Panopticon; prison; prison privatisation; prison reform; punishment

Møller, Bjørn. *Refugees, Prisoners and Camps: A Functional Analysis of the Phenomenon of Encampment.* Basingstoke: Palgrave Macmillan, 2015. DOI: 10.1057/9781137502797.0006.

DOI: 10.1057/9781137502797.0006

Prisons and similar camp-like institutions are found in most modern societies in which they are held to be valuable means of ensuring society and citizens against crime, or the state as such against insurgency – either in the sense of deterring law-breaking, of transforming miscreants into law-abiding citizens or simply of separating trouble-makers from the rest of society, thereby protecting the latter against the former.

2.1   The pros and cons of punishment

Even though the two are often conflated – not so much in the criminological and penological literature as in the public debate – the punitive and preventative functions are both conceptually and theoretically quite different.[1] It is, of course, possible to make an argument to the effect that punishment may help prevent certain acts, either through general or individual deterrence or both. It is thus prima facie plausible that observing that fellow citizens are punished for particular acts, for example, by having to serve lengthy prison sentences (and perhaps especially under harsh conditions), may make other people think twice about behaving in the same fashion and then reaching the conclusion that the potential gains do not justify the risks. However, the empirical evidence offers very little support of this kind of general deterrence.[2] It may also seem plausible that a first-time offender sentenced to incarceration may be deterred by his or her prison experience from misbehaving in the future (i.e., imprisonment should reduce recidivism), but again the empirical evidence does not really support this hypothesis of individual deterrence.[3]

As argued by prison reformers such as Jeremy Bentham and his present-day successors, it may also be possible to transform criminals, deviants and anti-socials into useful citizens by means of various aspects of imprisonment besides that of the deprivation of freedom. Bentham thus went to great length to actually design a prison with this objective in mind: his famous 'Panopticon,' that is, a prison in which the architectural outline ensured that the inmates either were under constant surveillance of the guards (who were themselves invisible) or at least felt constantly observed (see Figure 2.1).

This constant gaze would presumably not only make them behave better while under surveillance, but also accustom, habituate and socialise them to better behaviour, even when the watchful eye was no longer there.[4]

DOI: 10.1057/9781137502797.0006

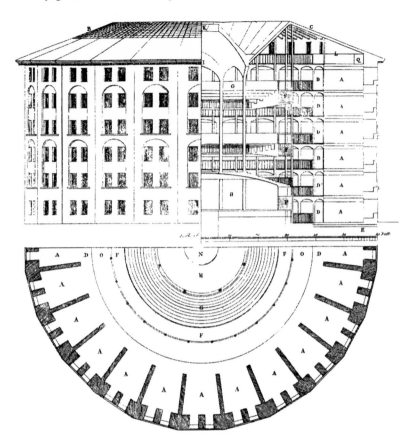

FIGURE 2.1   *Panopticon*

Source: J. Bentham (1838) 'Panopticon or, The Inspection House,' in *The Works of Jeremy Bentham*, IV (Edinburgh: William Tait), 172 available at the Online Library of Liberty. (http://lf-oll.s3.amazonaws.com/titles/1925/0872.04_Bk.pdf).

This notion certainly has its merits and its inherent logic may even be extended. Several religions are thus based on the assumption that we are all being constantly watched by none other than God himself, who meticulously keeps track of our (mis)behaviour and eventually passes judgement on us, either upon our individual death, sentencing us to spend eternity either in Hell or in Paradise, perhaps after a temporary sojourn in the Purgatory – or on the terrible Day of Judgement/Wrath, known from the *Dies Irae* section of the Catholic liturgy's Requiem mass. On this day, *Liber scriptum proferetur in quo totem continetur, unde mundus*

DOI: 10.1057/9781137502797.0006

iudicetur' ('a book is proffered in which everything is contained, on the basis of which the world will be judged').[5] Once again, while one might think that this would make believers behave better than[1] atheists or agnostics, the empirical evidence does not seem to support this assumption. For instance, Catholics (who are expected to believe in the importance of good deeds) do not seem to behave significantly better than Protestants who are explicitly *not* supposed to believe in the redeeming consequences of such deeds.[6]

The Panopticon idea has also been extended to general surveillance in society where it may, according to Foucault and others, enhance governmentality.[7] An early instance of this was the various attempts by city planners and architects to make Paris more 'transparent' as a contribution to (what we would today label as) urban counter-insurgency. Partly drawing on his own experiences from the 1830/1832 and 1848 revolutions in the French capital, the aforementioned novelist Victor Hugo in *Les Miserables* described the effect of darkness in a Parisian *faubourg* during the 1832 revolution, and how it benefited the insurgents:

> Thanks to the broken lanterns, thanks to the closed windows, there all radiance, all life, all sound, all movement ceased. The invisible police of the insurrection were on the watch everywhere, and maintained order, that is to say, night. The necessary tactics of insurrection are to drown small numbers in a vast obscurity, to multiply every combatant by the possibilities which that obscurity contains. At dusk, every window where a candle was burning received a shot. The light was extinguished, sometimes the inhabitant was killed.[8]

Hence the imperative for the restored monarchical regime to illuminate the city, including the 'dangerous neighbourhoods,' by installing street lights and by, as far as possible, replacing the curved and easily barricaded alleys with straight boulevards.[9]

Today's urban areas are, similarly, constantly surveilled and thus influenced by the growing 'panopticism,' to which a large and rapidly growing body of research is devoted.[10] One of the main components of this contemporary panopticism is the proliferation of closed-circuit-television (CCTV) installations around the world's urban congregations.[11] One might also include the fact that virtually everybody today walks around with a ready-for-use camera with a built-in capacity for rapid and wide dissemination, in the form of their cell- or smart phones in combination with media such as Facebook and YouTube – with

DOI: 10.1057/9781137502797.0006

the implication that just about everybody may find a picture of themselves in an embarrassing or compromising situation in cyberspace, a phenomenon sometimes referred to as 'lateral' or 'peer-to-peer surveillance' or even '*souveillance*'.[12] Although one might have expected this phenomenon to have significantly affected the behaviour of citizens – as measured by, for instance, crime rates – this does not actually seem to be the case.[13]

Institutions as psychiatric clinics, hospitals and other places of confinement also serve to contain dissent and divergence from the prevailing norms – as argued by Foucault in his work on *Madness and Civilization*:

> The walls of confinement actually enclose the negative of that moral city of which the bourgeois conscience began to dream in the seventeenth century; a moral city for those who sought, from the start, to avoid it; a city where right reigns only by virtue of a force without appeal – a sort of sovereignty of good (...). In the shadows of the bourgeois city is born this strange republic of the good which is imposed by force on all those suspected of belonging to evil.[14]

Another reason for incarcerating criminals and others is to keep them 'out of circulation' according to the reasonable assumption that as long as they are locked up, they will abstain from misbehaving. This may well be true – even though a gangster boss can in some cases run his criminal organisation from behind bars – but making this the basis for imprisonment policies tends to produce very large prison populations.[15] For a list of especially large prison populations, see Table 2.1. The source of these statistics also shows a very great variation in imprisonment rates, also between otherwise quite similar countries. The number of prison inmates per 100,000 inhabitants in the USA is thus almost seven times that of Canada, in Estonia almost five times that of Finland and in Sri Lanka almost four times that of India. The United States has, by far, the largest prison population of the world, also on a per capita basis, followed by China and Russia and other parts of what used to be the USSR. Even though it does not really influence global figures, it is also striking that the tiny island states in the Caribbean have very high percentages of their populations behind bars.[16]

Some have suggested solving the 'prison crisis', especially in the United States, through outsourcing, that is, privatisation.[17] This may either take the form of a private company (e.g., G4S) performing contractually specified tasks for the state such as transporting, housing and catering for the inmates,[18] or it may go one step further by also

TABLE 2.1 *Prison populations: the top ten*

Absolute Numbers

	Europe		N. America		Lat. America/Carib.		Africa		Asia & Pacific	
1	Russia	806,100	USA	2,292,133	Brazil	496,251	S. Africa	159,265	China	1,650,000
2	Ukraine	154,027	Canada	39,132	Mexico	222,330	Ethiopia	85,450	India	384,753
3	Turkey	124,074	Berm.	278	Columbia	84,444	Nigeria	50,000	Thail.	224,292
4	UK	94,461	Greenl.	194	Argentina	60,611	Rwanda	62,000	Iran	220,000
5	Poland	83,401			Chile	52,563	Kenya	49,757	Indon.	117,863
6	Spain	73,459			Peru	47,164	Egypt	64,378	Vietnam	108,557
7	Germ.	69,385			Venezuela	43,461	Morocco	61,405	Philipp.	102,267
8	Italy	67,615			El Salv.	24,283	Algeria	58,000	Pakistan	75,586
9	France	59,655			Dom. R.	21,050	Tanzania	40,000	Japan	74,476
10	Belarus	36,533			Panama	12,293	Tunisia	31,000	Banglad.	69,650

Per 100,000 Inhabitants center and boldface

	Europe		N. America		Lat. America/Carib.		Africa		Asia & Pacific	
1	Russia	568	USA	743	VI (US)	539	Rwanda	595	Palau	378
2	Georgia	547	Berm.	428	SK & N	495	S. Africa	316	Kazakh.	351
3	Belarus	381	Greenl.	340	VI (UK)	468	Tunisia	297	Maldives	343
4	Ukraine	338	Canada	117	Belize	439	Botswana	267	Thailand	328
5	Latvia	314			Grenada	423	Cape V.	253	Israel	319
6	Lithuania	276			Curacao	422	Swaziland	219	Guam	318
7	Estonia	254			El Salvador	391	Libya	203	Iran	291
8	Azerb.	228			Anquila	387	Gabon	196	Singapore	265
9	Monten.	227			Baham.	382	Morocco	189	Taiwan	278
10	CR./Pol.	218			SV&G	379	Namibia	186	Mongolia	269

Source: International Centre for Prison Studies (2011) *World Prison Population List. 9th ed.*, www.prisonstudies.org/images/news_events/wppl9.pdf.

Legend: VI: Virgin Islands; SK&N: St. Kitts & Nevis; SV&G: St. Vincent & Grenadines; Cape V: Cape Verde; CR: Czech Republic.

allowing for the exploitation of prison labour 'for profit.'[19] Some would, for principled reasons, oppose any such outsourcing of what are, allegedly by their very nature, public tasks,[20] whereas others (including the present author) would take a more pragmatic view, for example, arguing that privatisation (if properly implemented) might reduce costs[21] to which they might add that prisons have in the past often been private. Some countries have gone quite far in this direction whereas others have not,[22] so it seems premature to conclude much from the experience so far.

Finally, we have the 'just desert' (also known as 'retributivist') argument for incarceration, which comes in different versions.[23] Either it amounts to society's revenge against criminals, for which no utilitarian or consequentialist arguments are required; or it is a concession to either the victims[24] or the general public, whose sentiments allegedly need to be accommodated – what may be called 'penal populism' as a concession to 'popular punitiveness.'[25]

2.2   Camps as prisons

Even though we have today come to regard imprisonment almost as the 'default mode' of punishment (viz. Foucault's 'self-evident character of prison punishment'[26]), it was rather rare both in Antiquity, throughout the Middle Ages and well into the early modern era.[27]

The lack of enthusiasm by the authorities for this penal form was partly due to the relatively high costs of maintaining reasonably escape-proof facilities and catering for their inmates, combined with the constant shortage of funds in the public purse. Occasionally, however, entrepreneurial businessmen could find ways of making the running of prisons profitable, for example, by keeping expenses on food to a minimum while charging high fees and using the inmates for forced labour. Hence, some prisons were private well into the modern period,[28] but occasionally the state also found ways to exploit the labour of prisoners, for example, in 'houses of correction' or '*Zuchthäuser*' which were usually workhouses[29] – or it might commute prison sentences into labour contracts, for example, in the navy, the ships then serving as a special kind of prisons in which the living conditions were no better (often worse) than ordinary prisons ashore.[30] Even in the Middle Ages, when prisons were mainly used for economic crimes such as defaulting on debts, either to the

DOI: 10.1057/9781137502797.0006

crown or (more rarely) to other citizens, prison wardens were somehow able to make money out of their functions, the evidence being that they were willing to pay quite handsomely for the assignment and were subsequently able to lease it to others. Some of the income derived from fees paid by the inmates, but there were surely other forms of income as well.[31]

To the extent that imprisonment was used, there seems to have been a gradual, but quite late, shift in the predominant rationale for the use of this sanction from custodial via punitive to correctional. For most of the medieval period, imprisonment or incarceration was rarely thought of as punishment so much as temporary custody, until a court of law had decided on the appropriate punishment.[32] With the growing humanism of the Renaissance and Enlightenment, however, it came to be seen as a preferable (punitive or retributional) substitute for capital or corporal punishment.[33] One of the most prominent advocates of an abolition of the death penalty was Cesare Beccaria (1738–1794) whose *Essay on Crimes and Punishment* (1764) made quite an impression in Enlightenment Europe, not least on Voltaire (1694–1778), and which was quite unequivocal in its condemnation:

> The punishment of death is pernicious to society, from the example of barbarity it affords. If the passions, or the necessity of war, have taught men to shed the blood of their fellow creatures, the laws, which are intended to moderate the ferocity of mankind, should not increase it by examples of barbarity, the more horrible as this punishment is usually attended with formal pageantry. Is it not absurd, that the laws, which detest and punish homicide, should, in order to prevent murder, publicly commit murder themselves? (...) What are the natural sentiments of every person concerning the punishment of death? We may read them in the contempt and indignation with which every one looks on the executioner, who is nevertheless an innocent executor of the public will, a good citizen, who contributes to the advantage of society, the instrument of the general security within, as good soldiers are without.[34]

As a next step, this rationale gradually and partly gave way to a correctional ambition, that is, it shifted from that of deliberately inflicting suffering on a felon, commensurate with his or her crime, to that of using confinement as a means to put criminals back onto 'the straight and narrow path' of virtue and law-abidance.[35]

As a companion to this trend, the modern era also saw the emergence of 'penology' as a scientific discipline, devoted to the study of

DOI: 10.1057/9781137502797.0006

punishment, with the aforementioned Bentham as one of the first authors to approach the topic from a scholarly point of view.[36] Himself to some extent inspired by the prominent British prison reformer, John Howard (1727–1790),[37] Bentham also became known for his involvement in, and inspiration for, prison reform, both in his home country and in Europe, and for having conceived of the aforementioned 'Panopticon.'

Ironically, among the advocates of an abolition of the death penalty, we also find two individuals whose names later came to be closely associated with an almost frivolous use of the death penalty: Maximilien Robespierre, the Jacobine dictator, and the physician Joseph-Ignace Guillotin (1738–1814), who advocated (but did not, as often assumed, actually invent) the instrument of decapitation named after him as more humane than the sword or the axe.[38] Notwithstanding the temporary surge of capital punishment during the French Revolution, however, the overall trend was towards a more sparing use of the death penalty in the modern period, even though most countries opted for retaining it as the ultimate legal sanction.[39]

The seventeenth century thus saw a growth of the prison system,[40] labelled 'the great confinement' by Foucault, who pointed out that prisons were only one among several institutions of confinement, along with so-called 'hospitals,' the purpose of which was not so much medical, that is, curing the sick as to promote 'order.' This was, for instance, the case of the huge *Hôpital Generale* in Paris, founded in 1656, which was 'not a medical establishment. It is rather a sort of semi-judicial structure, an administrative entity which, along with the already constituted powers, and outside of the courts, decides, judges and executes.'[41]

Prisons were generally miserable places, inter alia because of very lax inspection systems and poor training of the personnel, but gradually the prison reformers managed to make them somewhat more hospitable. Following Norbert Elias (1897–1990), one may thus see this entire process from the frequent use of capital and corporal punishment via the use of punitive imprisonment to incarceration for the sake of correction as an integral element of the civilisation process, 'trickling down' through all layers of society.[42] This was at least compatible with the hypothesis of the French sociologist Durkheim of a 'penal evolution' towards less draconian punishment, and manifested in a decline of capital and corporeal punishment, as a companion of the growing differentiation of society.[43] We might also mention the German philosopher G.W.F. Hegel who in his *Philosophy of Right* described the evolution from revenge to punishment

DOI: 10.1057/9781137502797.0006

as part of the civilisational evolution from a system based on individual to the collective will, that is, from right (understood as entitlement) to morality.[44]

A very special contemporary case of camp-prisons is that of Guantanamo, which has aptly been described as 'a prison beyond the law' and as a 'legal black hole.'[45] First of all, it is (surely deliberately) located outside normal US jurisdiction, on a US Naval Base on territory leased from Cuba. The site had previously been used as a holding area for boat refugees from Haiti in 1993 until this was declared unconstitutional. Second, the inmates have never been sentenced to any form of incarceration, but they are merely suspected of involvement in international terrorism. Third, it remains unclear or undecided which set of laws they are suspected of having violated, as they have been granted status neither as prisoners-of-war nor as ordinary criminals, but they are referred to as 'unlawful combatants' – a home-made term for a category that appears neither in international law or US national law nor in international humanitarian law. This very dubious status of the indefinite incarceration of suspects has met with widespread criticism, but nothing had by the time of writing been done – even by the Obama administration – to rectify it (*vide infra*).

2.3   Punitive 'transportation'

Punishment may also involve removal ('transportation' in penological terms)[46] which may in turn be subdivided into removal *from* somewhere and *to* somewhere else.

From the first category we could mention the historical penalty of banishment.[47] The first recorded instance of this is, of course, that of Adam and Eve from the Garden of Eden for eating an apple from the forbidden tree (*Genesis* 3:23), followed by the banishment of their son Cain, who was made 'a restless wanderer on the earth' for the crime of fratricide, that is, the killing of his brother Abel (*Genesis* 4: 12–16). In Ancient Greece banishment was commonly known as 'ostracism,' and it was used quite extensively, also for political offences.[48] In both republican and imperial Rome, exile was, similarly, used frequently, often as an alternative to capital punishment.[49] The same was the case of medieval Europe, where one of the most famous victims was Dante Alighieri (1265–1321), who in his *magnum opus*, the *Divine Comedy* described the sufferings incurred from being banished from his beloved Florence:

> Thou shalt abandon everything beloved
>
> Most tenderly, and this the arrow is
>
> Which first the bow of banishment shoots forth.
>
> Thou shalt have proof how savoureth of salt
>
> The bread of others, and how hard a road
>
> The going down and up another's stairs.[50]

In modern times, the USSR has resorted to the banishment of critics, among whom we find the literary Nobel laureate Alexander Solzhenitsyn who was deported and banished from his motherland in 1974, and deprived of his Soviet citizenship as punishment for having written (but not yet published) *The Gulag Archipelago*, to which we shall return shortly. Others, such as the nuclear physicist and regime critic Andrei Sakharov were sentenced, like Dante, to internal exile.[51]

In medieval times the banishment from a city where a culprit had committed a crime was quite common, but it was also possible to ban a convict from 'civilised society' as such, thus depriving him (or, less frequently, her) of enjoyment of 'the King's peace.' The unfortunate then became what the Italian philosopher Giorgio Agamben, resurrecting from oblivion a Roman law concept, called a *homo sacer*, that is, 'sacred man,' who could be killed with impunity, but not sacrificed to the gods. S/he was thus condemned to 'living in a zone of indistinction situated between the *zoë*, the natural life common to humans, Gods, and animals, and the *bios* which is the life proper to humans,' and as 'an obscure figure of archaic Roman law in which human life is included in the juridical order (...) solely in the form of exclusion (i.e.,, of its capacity to be killed).'[52] The *homo sacer* was thus an outlaw. By placing persons convicted of a crime beyond the bounds of the law, they were at the mercy of every member of society – in effect forcing them to perpetuate a life of crime, which has sometimes been romanticised – most famously in the Robin Hood myth or the mythology surrounding the pirates.[53] The German term for outlaw, *vogelfrei* (literally 'free as a bird') is almost synonymous with the term *friedlos* ('without peace') and contains the same dualism, which has indeed fascinated authors such as Friedrich Nietzsche.[54]

The Catholic church commanded an equivalent, but perhaps even more deterring, form of punishment in the form of excommunication.[55]

DOI: 10.1057/9781137502797.0006

Whereas for protestants this would not necessarily be all that frightening thanks to the aforementioned doctrine(s) of *sola fide/sola gratia*, according to which faith and grace were the only routes to redemption, which the church could neither grant nor deny.[56] The Catholic faith, however, includes the doctrine of *extra ecclesia nullum salus* ('no salvation outside the church'), implying that excommunication is ipso facto tantamount to eternal damnation.[57] The threat of excommunication was thus a very serious one indeed which could be used against everybody, from the lowliest peasants to kings or even emperors – as when the Emperor of the Holy Roman Empire, Henry IV (1050–1106), in 1077 was forced to walk barefoot all the way to Canossa and stand in the snow for three entire days to atone his 'sins' (mainly that of insubordination to church authority) and in return have his excommunication revoked by Pope Gregory VII (c. 1020–1085).[58]

2.4 Deportation and penal colonies

Although the above refers to people being banned *from* their home cities, regions, countries or communities, leaving them free to decide on their whereabouts, in other cases convicts have been banned *to* special locations.

In some cases, state or imperial territories have encompassed locations so remote and/or inaccessible that they could serve as penal colonies, occasionally even without constructing any walls or fences. Islands are, for obvious reasons, often suitable for this purpose.[59] After his defeat the French Emperor Napoleon Bonaparte was thus (by the Treaty of Fontainebleau) banished to the island of Elba, 12 nautical miles off the coast of Tuscany. Allowed to retain his title of Emperor and even granted sovereign power over the small island, he was able to escape in 1815. Following his 'Hundred Days' he was exiled to another island, this time the much more remote and inaccessible St. Helena in the Atlantic Ocean off the African coast where he resided for the rest of his life, 1815–1821.[60] The camp was later used by the British for prisoners of war from the Boer War (*vide infra*).[61] One of the most (in)famous of the French penal colonies was the so-called '*Île du Diable*' (Devil's Island) forming part of the small '*Îles du Salut*' (Salvation Island) off mainland French Guiana,[62] which numbered among its involuntary inhabitants the victim of the Dreyfus Affair, the Jewish captain in the French army, Alfred Dreyfus.[63]

DOI: 10.1057/9781137502797.0006

The British also made use of an island as recipient of their convicts, albeit a much larger one, namely Australia.[64] Portugal, similarly, used their South American (Brazil) and later African colonies such as Angola as penal colonies.[65] More recently, the apartheid regime of South Africa used a former leper colony and lunatic asylum,[66] Robben Island (off Cape Town) as a penal colony for its political opponents, mainly from the ANC (African National Congress), hosting, among others, the late Nelson Mandela.[67]

In Russia and the Soviet Union, the vastness of the national territory made the resort to islands superfluous, as the vast distances and the inhospitable climate in some of the most remote regions made escape practically impossible, or at least practically suicidal. Imperial Russia nevertheless used the Sakhalin Island as a penal outpost, described by the famous physician and playwright, Anton Chekov, who visited it in preparation of his medical doctorate and subsequently described the miserable conditions of the deportees.[68] More often, however, Czarist Russia used Siberia for its terrestrial prison and labour camps,[69] known inter alia from Dostoyevsky's *Memories from the House of the Dead* as well as Tolstoy's *Resurrection*.[70]

In this practice they were emulated by their Bolshevik successors in the Soviet Union, who expanded the system immensely into what has become known as the 'Gulag Archipelago,'[71] partly known as such from the works of a former inmate, the aforementioned Solzhenitsyn.[72] The term 'GULAG' was an acronym for *Glavnoe Upravlenie Lagerei*, that is, 'Main Camp Administration.' More than other penal colonies, this vast system served a dual purpose, that is, to incarcerate political opponents and to exploit their labour under slave-like conditions. Most of the 'political' opponents were categorised and treated as such on pseudo-scientific 'objective' criteria in the sense that successful peasants were labelled as 'Kulaks' and ipso facto categorised and punished as political opponents.[73] The ranks of 'political opponents' were thus often replenished by quota, in the sense that the secret police, NKVD (*Narodnyy Komissariat Vnutrennikh Del*, i.e., People's Commissariat for Internal Affairs), and its successors were tasked with apprehending a specified number of 'opponents,' who were then exploited for hard manual labour under life-threatening working conditions. Notwithstanding the utter ruthlessness with which convicts were employed,[74] however, the Soviet authorities seem to never have really succeeded in making the system economically viable,[75] even though it

DOI: 10.1057/9781137502797.0006

did help 'opening up' the arctic parts of the USSR.[76] While most camps were ringed with barbed wire fences and the like, the most remote ones were usually not, as their very location appeared to suffice for discouraging escape.[77] One strategy for escape from the most remote camps was, however, for two inmates to team up and invite a third to join them in the escape, but in reality mainly serving as a 'walking food reserve.'[78]

In the camps a hierarchy developed between the various categories of prisoners, with the professional criminals at the apex, followed by the politicals and with the common criminals and 'anti-socials' at the bottom. There was some 'social mobility,' even between Gulag inmates and guards, some inmates being included in the staff and some guards sentenced to incarceration.[79] At the very bottom of the prison hierarchy were the totally emaciated and dying, referred to as *dokhodyagi*, quite similar to the *Muselmänner* of the Nazi concentration camps (see Chapter 3).[80] Much more frequently than in the Nazi camps, there were rebellions (sometimes taking the form of strikes) and escape attempts. Other similarities notwithstanding, the Communists seemingly never sought to transform the system into a killing machinery, as did the Nazis with their extermination camps (see Chapter 3). Even though the death-toll was enormous, it seems to have been predominantly inadvertent, that is, a tolerated side-effect of the economic endeavour. Moreover, all inmates were sentenced to incarceration, even though these sentences were, of course, arrived at through a profoundly flawed legal process, featuring extensive use of torture.

The German attack on the 22 June 1941, however, resulted in a strictly administrative prolongation of all sentences for the politicals, who were to remain in the camps for the duration of the war, in the course of which living conditions dramatically deteriorated and the mortality rate rose steeply,[81] both because of the general strains of the war on the economy and because of the massive increase of the camp population. Most of these new arrivals were incarcerated administratively, in some cases even the result of the mass deportation of nationalities deemed dangerous.[82] The total camp population of the USSR was also increased by the addition of prisoners-of-wars (POWs) (*vide infra*) who were sometimes also put up in existing Gulag camps – not only those of the Germans and their allied who had surrendered to the Red Army, but also those who had surrendered to the Western allies and then been repatriated to their Soviet homeland, but who were suspected of illoyality by the Stalinist

DOI: 10.1057/9781137502797.0006

regime and therefore interned in the Gulag.[83] Although the consequence of all these measures was to increase camp population, what limited this increase was a major, but partial, amnesty with the outbreak of the war, the net result of which seems to have been a decline in total camp population.[84]

Although the Soviet Gulag was largely dismantled after the death of Joseph Stalin, according to some observers the bizarre communist dictatorship of North Korea (formally called the Democratic People's Republic of Korea, DPRK) has until the present day maintained a similar Gulag, mainly for political prisoners.[85] In February 2014, the UN's Human Rights Council thus published a highly incriminating major report on human rights violations in the DPRK, including satellite images of the main *kwanliso* camps for political prisoners, as opposed to the *kyohwaso* camps for ordinary criminals. Most of these camps, similar to their Soviet precursors, apparently serve the dual function of deterring the opposition by punishing political opponents and exploiting their forced labour. The same has been the case of Eritrea, where conscription (with the world's probably longest conscription periods) has been used as a framework for forced labour – referred to as the *Warsai-Yikealo* programme, launched in 2002 – partly organised in camps such as the notorious Sawa camp, and, according to most analyses, hugely ineffective.[86]

Although these labour camps presupposed keeping the workforce fenced *in*, it is also possible to exploit a population which is systematically kept *out*. Apartheid South Africa probably offers the best illustrations of this, where the shantytowns, townships and later homelands ('Bantustans')[87] were intended as the permanent residence of the workforce who were either 'allowed' on a daily basis to enter the white residential areas to work, administratively regulated by the notorious 'pass laws,'[88] or occasionally permitted to stay for longer period in the infamous hostels closer to their places of work.[89] While this was a matter of keeping the less fortunate fellow citizens out, another form of segregation between the haves and the have-nots of societies is the establishment of the aforementioned 'gated communities' of which there are many in the more affluent (and predominantly white) parts of a country such as South Africa.[90] The phenomenon is, however universal, the United States having lots of such enclosures, which is also the case of other western countries,[91] as well as cities (and, not least, megacities) all across the Third World.[92]

DOI: 10.1057/9781137502797.0006

2.5 Summary

We have thus seen that punishment can serve several functions (revenge, general and specific deterrence and correction) in different societies at different times, and that imprisonment, which is today almost viewed as the default form of punishment, is actually a fairly new phenomenon. Its main function is the separation of the deviants from the normal population in order to protect the latter from the former. This can also be accomplished by such institutions as mental and other hospitals, or by deportation (often referred to as 'transportation'), either to distant and usually inhospitable parts of the country or to prison colonies on inaccessible islands. Such deportation may also be economically motivated, even though the historical evidence points to many obstacles standing in the way of making forced labour in prison/work camps profitable – as was also the case in the Nazi concentration camps, as we shall see in the next chapter.

Notes

1. J. Bentham (1838) 'Principles of Penal Law', in *The Works of Jeremy Bentham* (n. 10) IV, 365–560, especially 'The Rationale of Punishment', 388–532; G. de Beaumont and A. de Tocqueville (1979) *On the Penitentiary System in the United States and Its Application in France* (Carnondale, SI: Southern Illinois University Press); M. Cavadino and J. Dignan (2007) *The Penal System: An Introduction*. 4th ed. (London: Sage), 35–65: T. Newburn (2007) *Criminology* (Portland, OR: Willan Publishing), 515–538.

2. G. Kleck et al. (2005) 'The Missing link in General Deterrence Research', *Criminology*, 43:3, 623–658; A. Von Hirsch et al. (1999) *Criminal Deterrence: An Analysis of Recent Research* (Oxford: Hart); A. Ashworth (2007) 'Sentencing', in M. Maguire et al. (eds.) *The Oxford Handbook of Criminology*. 4th ed. (Oxford: Oxford University Press), 990–1023, especially 993–994.

3. F.T. Cullen et al. (2011) 'Prisons Do Not Reduce Recidivism: The High Costs of Ignoring Science', *Prison Journal*, 91:3, Supplement, 48S–65S; M. Windzio (2006) 'Is there a Deterrent Effect of Pains of Imprisonment? The Impact of 'Social Costs' of First Incarceration on the Hazard Rate of Recidivism', *Punishment and Society*, 8:3, 341–364. On the American 'three strikes policy' see J. Austin et al. (1999) 'The Impact of 'Three Strikes and You're Out', ibid., 1:2, 131–162; D. Shichor (1997) 'Three Strikes as a Public Policy: The Convergence of the New Penology and the McDonaldization of Punishment', *Crime and Delinquency*, 43:4, 470–492.

DOI: 10.1057/9781137502797.0006

4   J. Bentham (1838) 'Panopticon' (n. 10), figure from p. 172; R.A. Cooper (1981)
     'Jeremy Bentham, Elizabeth Fry, and English Prison Reform,' *Journal of the
     History of Ideas*, 42:4, 675–690; H. Strub (1989) 'The Theory of Panoptical
     Control: Bentham's Panopticon and Orwell's Nineteen Eighty-Four,' *Journal
     of the History of the Behavioral Sciences*, 25, 40–59. The classical critique of this
     is M. Foucault (1991), *Discipline and Punish: The Birth of the Prison* (London:
     Penguin), 195–228.

5   Based mainly on *Revelation* 20:12.

6   See art. 20 of the *Augsburg Confession*, at www.logia.org/pdf/augsburg.pdf; or
     John Calvin 'On Justification by Faith' at www.ondoctrine.com/2calo501.htm.
     See also T. Peters (2002) 'Grace, Doubt, and Evil: The Constructive Task of
     Reformation Theology,' *Dialog: A Journal of Theology*, 41:4, 273–284.

7   Foucault, *Discipline and Punish* (n. 4), 195–228.

8   V. Hugo, *Les Miserables*, 4:13, 2. English translation at www.gutenberg.org/
     files/135/135-h/135-h.htm#link2HCH0286.

9   W. Schivelbusch (1987) 'The Policing of Street Lighting,' *Yale French Studies*,
     73, 61–74; W. Benjamin (2004) 'Paris, Capital of the Nineteenth Century,' in
     C. Jenks (ed.) *Urban Culture: Critical Concepts in Literary and Cultural Studies*
     (London: Taylor and Francis), 239–254, especially p. 248; M. Pensky (2005)
     'Memory, Catastrophe, Destruction,' *City*, 9:2, 205–214; D.P. Jordan (2004)
     'Hausmann and Hausmannisation: The Legacy of Paris,' *French Historical
     Studies*, 27:1, 87–113; F. Bourillon (1999) 'Changer la ville. La question
     urbaine au millieu du 19e siècle,' *Vintième Sciecle*. 64, 11–23, especially 15–16.
     On modern times see N.K. Katyal (2002) 'Architecture as Crime Control,'
     Yale Law Journal, 111:5, 1039–1139; B.C. Welsh and D.P. Farrington (2004)
     'Surveillance for Crime Prevention in Public Space: Results and Policy
     Choices in Britain and America,' *Criminology and Public Policy*, 3:3, 497–526;
     idem and idem (2006) 'CCTV and Street Lightning: Comparative Effects on
     Crime,' in A.E. Perry et al. (eds.) *Reducing Crime: The Effectiveness of Criminal
     Justice Interventions* (London: John Wiley and Sons), 95–113.

10   N. Gane (2012) 'The Governmentalities of Neoliberalism: Panopticism,
     Post-Panopticism and Beyond,' *Sociological Review*, 60:4, 611–634; J.E. Dobson
     and P.F. Fisher (2007) 'The Panopticon's Changing Geography,' *Geographical
     Review*, 97:3, 307–323; M. Gray (2003) 'Urban Surveillance and Panopticism:
     Will We Recognize the Facial Recognition Society?' *Surveillance and Society*,
     1:3, 314–330.

11   B. Goold et al. (2013) 'The Banality of Security: The Curious Case of
     Surveillance Cameras,' *British Journal of Criminology*, 53:6, 977–996; I.R.
     Cook and M. Whowell (2011) 'Visibility and the Policing of Public Space,'
     Geography Compass, 5:8, 610–622; K.S. Williams and C. Johnstone (2000) 'The
     Politics of the Selective Gaze: Closed Circuit Television and the Policing of
     Public Space,' *Crime, Law and Social Change*, 34:2, 183–210.

DOI: 10.1057/9781137502797.0006

12   M. Andrejevic (2006) 'The Discipline of Watching: Detection, Risk, and Lateral Surveillance,' *Critical Studies in Media Communication*, 23:5, 391–407.

13   J. Chan (2008) 'The New Lateral Surveillance and a Culture of Suspicion,' *Sociology of Crime, Law and Deviance*, 10:2, 223–239.

14   M. Foucault (2001) *Madness and Civilization: A History of Insanity in the Age of Reason* (London: Routledge), 56–57.

15   A. Blumstein (2011) 'Bringing Down the U.S. Prison Population,' *Prison Journal*, 91:3, 12S–26S.

16   Based on International Centre for Prison Studies (2011) *World Prison Population List*. 9th ed., at www.prisonstudies.org/images/news_events/wppl9.pdf.

17   P.J. Duitsman (1998) 'The Private Prison Experiment: A Private Sector Solution to Prison Overcrowding,' *North Carolina Law Review*, 76:6, 2209–2265.

18   S. Armstrong (2002) 'Punishing Not-for-Profit: Implications of Nonprofit Privatization in Juvenile Punishment,' *Punishment and Society*, 4:3, 348–368.

19   R. White (1999) 'Prison Labour,' *Current Issues in Criminal Justice*, 11:2, 243–248; P.A. Ethridge and J.W. Marquart (1993) 'Private Prisons in Texas: The New Penology for Profits,' *Justice Quarterly*, 10:1, 29–48; C. Fenwick (2005) 'Private Use of Prisoners' Labor: Paradoxes of International Human Rights Law,' *Human Rights Quarterly*, 27:1, 249–293; M.A. Hallett (2002) 'Race, Crime, and For-Profit Imprisonment: Social Disorganization as Market Opportunity,' *Punishment and Society*, 4:3, 369–393.

20   M.D. Reisig and T.C. Pratt (2000) 'The Ethics of Correctional Privatization: A Critical Examination of the Delegation of Coercive Authority,' *Prison Journal*, 80:2, 210–222; E. Genders (2002) 'Legitimacy, Accountability and Private Prisons,' *Punishment and Society*, 4:3, 285–303; Y. Jing (2010) 'Prison Privatization: A Perspective on Core Governmental Functions,' *Crime, Law and Social Change*, 54:3–4, 263–278.

21   K.I. Avio (1991) 'On Private Prisons: An Economic Analysis of the Model Contract and Model Statute for Private Incarceration,' *New England Journal on Criminal and Civil Confinement*, 17:2, 265–300; D. Shichor (1999) 'Privatizing Correctional Institutions: An Organizational Perspective,' *Prison Journal*, 79:2, 226–249.

22   D.E. Pozen (2003) 'Managing a Correctional Marketplace: Prison Privatization in the United States and the United Kingdom,' *Journal of Law and Politics*, 19:1, 253–284.

23   Newburn, *Criminology* (n. 36), 524–527; Cavadino and Dignan, *The Penal System* (n. 1), 44–46.

24   D.N. Gromet (2012) 'Restoring the Victim: Emotional Reactions, Justice Beliefs, and Support for Reparation and Punishment,' *Critical Criminology*, 20:1, 9–23.

DOI: 10.1057/9781137502797.0006

25 J. Pratt (2008) 'Penal Populism and the Contemporary Role of Punishment,' in T. Anthony and C. Cunneen (eds.) *The Critical Criminology Companion* (Sydney: Hawkins Press), 265–276.

26 Foucault, *Discipline and Punish* (n. 4), 232.

27 E.M. Peters (1998): 'Prison before the Prisons: The Ancient and Medieval Worlds,' in N. Morris and D.J. Rothman (eds.) *Oxford History of the Prison* (Oxford: Oxford University Press) (n.10), 3–43; V. Hunter (1997): 'The Prison of Athens: A Comparative Perspective,' *Phoenix*, 51:3–4, 296–326; P. Spierenburg (1997) 'The Body and the State: Early Modern Europe,' ibid., 44–70; J. Dunbabin (2002) *Captivity and Imprisonment in Medieval Europe, 1000–1300* (Basingstoke: Palgrave Macmillan).

28 John A. Conley (1980) 'Prisons, Production, and Profit: Reconsidering the Importance of Prison Industries,' *Journal of Social History*, 14:2, 257–275; G. Hawkins (1983) 'Prison Labor and Prison Industries,' *Crime and Justice*, 5, 85–127; G. Rusche and O. Kirchheimer (2003) *Punishment and Social Structure* (Newark, NY: Transaction Publishers), 24–52.

29 J.F. Harrington (1999) 'Escape from the Great Confinement: The Genealogy of a German Workhouse,' *Journal of Modern History*, 71:2, 308–345.

30 G. Best (1998) *War and Society in Revolutionary Europe 1770–1870* (London: Sutton), 40.

31 M. Bassett (1944) 'The Fleet Prison in the Middle Ages,' *University of Toronto Law Journal*, 5:2, 383–402; idem (1943) 'Newgate Prison in the Middle Ages,' *Speculum*, 18:2, 233–246; R.W. Ireland (1987) 'Theory and Practice within the Medieval English Prison,' *American Journal of Legal History*, 31:1, 56–67.

32 J.L. Langbein (1976) 'The Historical Origins of the Sanction of Imprisonment for Serious Crime,' *Journal of Legal Studies*, 5:1, 35–60.

33 J.J. Megivern (1997) *The Death Penalty: An Historical and Theological Survey* (Mahwa, NJ: Paulist Press), 209–252.

34 C. Beccaria (1764, reprint 1819) *An Essay on Crimes and Punishment*, at www.constitution.org/cb/crim_pun.htm, quote from chapter 28. See also M. Maestro (1973) 'A Pioneer for the Abolition of Capital Punishment: Cesare Beccaria,' *Journal of the History of Ideas*, 34:3, 463–468. On Voltaire's advocacy of these ideas see V.W. Topazio (1959) 'Voltaire, Philosopher of Human Progress,' *PMLA*, 74:4, 356–364.

35 Z. Bauman (2000) 'Social Uses of Law and Order,' in D. Garland and R. Sparks (eds.) *Criminology and Social Theory* (Oxford: Oxford University Press), 23–46.

36 H.A. Bedau (1983) 'Bentham's Utilitarian Critique of the Death Penalty,' *Journal of Criminal Law and Criminology*, 74:3, 1033–1065.

37 R.A. Cooper (1976) 'Ideas and Their Execution: English Prison Reform,' *Eighteenth-Century Studies*, 10:1, 73–93; E. Stockdale (1983) 'A Short History of Prison Inspection in England,' *British Journal of Criminology*, 23:3, 209–228.

DOI: 10.1057/9781137502797.0006

38　On Robespierre's opposition to a retention of the death penalty in 1791 see pp. 506–507 in M. Maestro (1978) 'Lafayette as a Reformer of Penal Laws,' *Journal of the History of Ideas*, 39:3, 503–510. On Guillotin see C.F. Donegan (1990) 'Dr. Guillotin: Reformer and Humanitarian,' *Journal of the Royal Society of Medicine*, 83:10, 637–639.

39　F.E. Hartung (1952) 'Trends in the Use of Capital Punishment,' *Annals of the American Academy of Political and Social Science*, 284, 8–19.

40　G. Fischer (1995) 'The Birth of the Prison Retold,' *Yale Law Journal*, 104:6, 1235–1324.

41　Foucault, *Madness and Civilization* (n. 4), 37.

42　J. Pratt (1999) 'Norbert Elias and the Civilized Prison,' *British Journal of Sociology*, 50:2, 271–296; B. Vaughan (2000) 'The Civilizing Process and the Janus-Face of Modern Punishment,' *Theoretical Criminology*, 4:1, 71–91; P. Spirenburg (2004) 'Punishment, Power and History: Foucault and Elias,' *Social Science History*, 28:4, 607–636.

43　E. Durkheim (1992) 'Two Laws of Penal Evolution,' in M. Cane (ed.) *The Radical Sociology of Durkheim and Mauss* (London: Routledge), 21–49; R. Cotterrell (1999) *Emile Durkheim: Law in a Moral Domain* (Edinburgh: Edinburgh University Press), 82–100.

44　G.W.F. Hegel (1968). 'Grundlinien der Philosophie des Rechts, oder Naturrecht und Staatswissenschaft im Grundrisse,' *Hegel Studienausgabe*, 2 (Frankfurt a.m.: Fischer Bücherei), 124–125. See also P.J. Steinberger (1983) 'Hegel on Crime and Punishment,' *American Political Science Review*, 77:4, 858–870.

45　J. Margulies (2004) 'A Prison Beyond the Law,' *Virginia Quarterly Review*, 80:4, 37–55.

46　G. Rusche and O. Kirchheimer (2003) *Punishment and Social Structure* (Newark, NY: Transaction Publishers), 114–126; R. Kingston (2005) 'The Unmaking of Citizens: Banishment and the Modern Citizenship Regime in France,' *Citizenship Studies*, 9:1, 23–40.

47　L.H. Bowker (1980) 'Exile, Banishment and Transportation,' *International Journal of Offender Therapy and Comparative Criminology*, 24:1, 67–80; W.G. Snider (1998) 'Banishment: The History of Its Use and a Proposal for Its Abolition under the First Amendment,' *New England Journal on Criminal and Civil Confinement*, 24:2, 455–510; J. Bleichmar (1999) 'Deportation as Punishment: A Historical Analysis of the British Practice of Banishment and Its Impact on Modern Constitutional Law,' *Georgetown Immigration Law Journal*, 14:1, 115–164.

48　D. Kagan (1961) 'The Origins and Purposes of Ostracism,' *Hesperia*, 30:4, 393–401; A.R. Hands (1959) 'Ostraka and the Law of Ostracism – Some Possibilities and Assumptions,' *Journal of Hellenic Studies*, 79, 69–79; R. Gorman (1994) 'Poets, Playwrights, and the Politics of Exile and Asylum in Ancient Greece and Rome,' *International Journal of Refugee Law*, 6:3, 402–424.

DOI: 10.1057/9781137502797.0006

49   R.A. Baumann (1996) *Crime and Punishment in Ancient Rome* (London: Routledge), 6–8.

50   D. Alighieri: 'Paradiso,' at www.divinecomedy.org/divine_comedy. html, XVII:55–60. See also M.E. Wolfgang (1954) 'Political Crimes and Punishments in Renaissance Florence,' *Journal of Criminal Law, Criminology, and Police Science*, 44:5, 555–581.

51   J. Bergman (1992) 'Soviet Dissidents on the Russian Intelligentsia, 1956–1985: The Search for a Usable Past,' *Russian Review*, 51:1, 16–35.

52   G. Agamben (1998) *Homo Sacer: Sovereign Power and Bare Life* (Stanford, CA: Stanford University Press), 1 and 8. See also W. Walters (2002) 'Deportation, Expulsion, and the International Police of Aliens,' *Citizenship Studies*, 6:3, 265–292; B. Diken and C.B. Laustsen (2002) 'Zones of Indistinction: Security, Terror and Bare Life,' *Space and Culture*, 5:3, 290–307.

53   M.H. Keen (1987) *The Outlaws of Medieval Legend*. 2nd ed. (London: Routledge); R.H. Hilton (1958) 'The Origins of Robin Hood,' *Past and Present*, 14, 30–44.

54   F. Nietzsche 'Lieder des Prinzen Vogelfrei,' appendix to *Die fröhliche Wissenschaft* (Munich: Wilhelm Goldman Verlag, no year, *Gesammelte Werke*, 6), 345–359.

55   R.H. Helmholz (1994) 'Excommunication in Twelfth Century England,' *Journal of Law and Religion*, 11:1, 235–253; M. Tausiet (2003) 'Excluded Souls: The Wayward and Excommunicated in Counter-Reformation Spain,' *History*, 88:291, 437–450.

56   P. Melanchton (1530) *Augsburg Confession*, at www.evangelicallutheransynod. org/augsburgconfession/; or J. Calvin (1841) *Institutes of the Christian Religion*, (Philadelphia: Presbyterian Board of Publication) II: 50–62.

57   See 'The Church' and 'Excommunication' in *Catholic Encyclopedia*, at www. newadvent.org/cathen/.

58   I.S. Robinson (1979) 'Pope Gregory VII, the Princes and the *Pactum* 1077–1080,' *English Historical Review*, 94:373, 721–756; R.B. Hall (1997) 'Moral Authority as a Power Resource,' *International Organization*, 51:4, 591–622.

59   A. Anderson (2006) 'Islands of Exile: Ideological Motivation in Maritime Migration,' *Journal of Island and Coastal Archaeology*, 1:1, 33–47.

60   M.J. Thornton (1968) *Napoleon after Waterloo: England and the St. Helena Decision* (Stanford, CA: Stanford University Press).

61   S.A. Royle (1998) 'St Helena as a Boer Prisoner of War Camp, 1900–2: Information from the Alice Stopford Green Papers,' *Journal of Historical Geography*, 24:1, 53–68.

62   A. Miles (1988) *Devil's Island: Colony of the Damned* (Berkeley, CA: Ten Speed Press); S.A. Toth (2006) *Beyond Papillon: The French Overseas Penal Colonies 1854–1952* (Lincoln, NE: University of Nebraska Press).

DOI: 10.1057/9781137502797.0006

63 G.R. Whyte (2005) *The Dreyfus Affair: A Chronological History* (London: Palgrave Macmillan), *passim*; H. Arendt (1968) *The Origins of Totalitarianism* (New York: Harcourt), 89–120.

64 I. Duffield (1986) 'From Slave Colonies to Penal Colonies: The West Indian Convict Transportees to Australia,' *Slavery and Abolition*, 7:1, 25–45; L.L. Robson (1970) *The Convict Settlers of Australia: An Enquiry into the Origin and Character of the Convicts Transported to New South Wales and Von Diemen's Land 1787–1852* (Melbourne: Melbourne University Press); D. Neal (1987) 'Free Society, Penal Colony, Slave Society, Prison,' *Historical Studies*, 22:89, 497–518.

65 T.J. Coates (2001) *Convicts and Orphans: Forced and State-Sponsored Colonizers in the Portuguese Empire, 1550–1755* (Stanford, CA: Stanford University Press), 42–64.

66 H.J. Deacon (1996) 'Madness, Race and Moral Treatment: Robben Island Lunatic Asylum, Cape Colony, 1846–1890,' *History of Psychiatry*, 7:26, 287–297.

67 N.E. Alexander (1994) *Robben Island Prison Dossier, 1964–1974* (Cape Town: University of Cape Town); F. Buntman (2003) *Robben Island and Prisoner Resistance to Apartheid* (Cambridge: Cambridge University Press).

68 A. Chekov (2007) *A Journey to the End of the Russian Empire* (Harmondsworth: Penguin), 52–71.

69 A.A. Gentes (2005) 'Katorga: Penal Labor and Tsarist Russia,' in E-M. Stolberg (ed.) *The Siberian Saga: A History of Russia's Wild East* (Frankfurt a.M.: Verlag Peter Lang), 73–85.

70 F. Dostoïeffsky (1911) *The House of the Dead, or Prison Life in Siberia* (London: Everyman's Library); L. Tolstoy (1899) *Resurrection* (www.gutenberg.org/etext/1938).

71 A. Applebaum (2004) *Gulag: A History* (London: Penguin); K. Brown (2007) 'Out of Solitary Confinement: The History of the Gulag,' *Kritika*, 8:1, 67–103.

72 A.I. Solzhenitsyn (1998) *The Gulag Archipelago, 1918–1956: An Experiment in Literary Investigation*, I–III (Boulder, CO: Westview).

73 N. Werth (1999) 'A State against Its People: Violence, Repression, and Terror in the Soviet Union,' in S. Courtois et al. (eds.) *The Black Book of Communism: Crimes, Terror, Repression* (Cambridge, MA: Harvard University Press), 33–268; M. Lewin (1966) 'Who Was the Soviet Kulak?' *Soviet Studies*, 18:2, 189–212; L. Viola (1996) *Peasant Rebels under Stalin: Collectivization and the Culture of Peasant Resistance* (Oxford: Oxford University Press), 27, 39–42.

74 S.A. Barnes (2000) 'Researching Daily Life in the Gulag,' *Kritika*, 1:2, 377–390.

75 H. Hunter (1980) 'The Economic Costs of the GULag Archipelago,' *Slavic Review*, 39:4, 588–592; S. Rosefelde (1981) 'An Assessment of the Sources and Uses of Gulag Forced Labour 1929–56,' *Soviet Studies*, 33:1, 51–87.

76 P. Josephson (2011) 'Technology and the Conquest of the Soviet Arctic,' *Russian Review*, 70:3, 419–439.

DOI: 10.1057/9781137502797.0006

77   Applebaum, *Gulag* (n. 70), 93–94.
78   Ibid., 355–370.
79   Ibid., 261–283.
80   Ibid., 307–315.
81   Ibid., 373–380.
82   Ibid., 381–401.
83   Ibid., 394–396.
84   Ibid., 402–413.
85   C. Gershman (2013) 'A Voice from the North Korean Gulag,' *Journal of Democracy*, 24:2, 165–173; D. Hawk (2012) *The Hidden Gulag: Exposing North Korea's Prison Camps* (U.S. Committee for Human Rights in North Korea), at www.hrnk.org/uploads/pdfs/HRNK_HiddenGulag2_Web_5-18.pdf; S. Haggard and M. Noland (2012) 'Economic Crime and Punishment in North Korea,' *Political Science Quarterly*, 127:4, 659–683.
86   G. Kibreab (2009) *Eritrea: A Dream Deferred* (Oxford: James Currey), 19–20, 60–61; Human Rights Watch (2009) *Service for Life: State Repression and Indefinite Conscription in Eritrea* (New York: HRW).
87   M. Lipton (1972) 'Independent Bantustans?' *International Affairs*, 48:1, 1–19.
88   M. Savage (1986) 'The Imposition of Pass Laws on the African Population in South Africa, 1916–1984,' *African Affairs*, 85:339, 181–205; S. Terreblance (2002) *A History of Inequality in South Africa, 1652–2002* (Pietermaritzburg: University of Natal Press), 312–333.
89   A. Sitas (1996) 'The New Tribalism: Violence and Hostels,' *Journal of Southern African Studies*, 22:2, 235–248.
90   U. Jürgens and M. Gnad (2002) 'Gated Communities in South Africa – Experiences from Johannesburg,' *Environment and Planning B: Planning and Design*, 29:3, 337–353; K. Landman and M. Schönteich (2002) 'Urban Fortresses: Gated Communities as a Reaction to Crime,' *African Security Review*, 11:4, 71–85.
91   E.J. Blakely and M.G. Snyder (1997) *Fortress America: Gated Communities in the United States* (Washington, DC: Brookings Institution); R.W. Helsey and W.C. Strange (1999) 'Gated Communities and the Economic Geography of Crime,' *Journal of Urban Economics*, 46:1, 80–105.
92   M. Coy and M. Pöhler (2002) 'Gated Communities in Latin American Megacities: Case Studies in Brazil and Argentina,' *Environment and Planning B: Planning and Design*, 29:3, 355–370; G. Glasze and A. Alkhayyal (2002) 'Gated Housing Estates in the Arab World: Case Studies in Lebanon and Riyadh, Saudi Arabia,' ibid., 321–336; H. Leisch (2002) 'Gated Communities in Indonesia,' *Cities*, 19:5, 341–350.

DOI: 10.1057/9781137502797.0006

3

Concentration Camps
and Ghettos

Abstract: *Chapter 3 offers a historical account of concentration camps from the very first, established in colonial settings, via the Nazi concentration camps to modern equivalents, for example, in North Korea. It also provides a classification of the Nazi concentration camps, including 'death factories' such as Auschwitz, and the perpetrators of genocide such as concentration camp guards, Einsatzgruppen and Nazi doctors such as Josef Mengele. Functional equivalents of industrialised mass murder such as slave labour and death marches are also covered as are post-war concentration camps.*

Keywords: Auschwitz; Bauman; Boer War; concentration camps; Eichmann; *Einsatzgruppen*; genocide; ghettos; Holocaust; Jewish Councils; Mengele

Møller, Bjørn. *Refugees, Prisoners and Camps: A Functional Analysis of the Phenomenon of Encampment.* Basingstoke: Palgrave Macmillan, 2015. DOI: 10.1057/9781137502797.0007.

Even though the term 'concentration camp' has now become, in the public mind at least, primarily associated with the German genocide of the Jews during World War II, with 'Auschwitz' as the epitome, neither the term nor the phenomenon are of German origin, and even the German concentration camps were a very amorphous bunch of camps with very diverse functions. Indeed, as we shall see shortly, even Auschwitz itself did not quite fit the paradigm as it was actually a mixed camp for forced labour (viz. the infamous sign at the entrance '*Arbeit macht Frei*') and extermination, the latter primarily relegated to the camp annex, Birkenau or 'Auschwitz II.'[1]

The first (but today almost forgotten) concentration camps seem to have been those (called '*reconcendrados*') built by Spain in Cuba in the wars 1868–1878, 1879–1880 and 1895–1898, and those established by the United States in the Philippines in 1898.[2] They were followed by the camps established in the Boer War by the British,[3] whose camps provoked a humanitarian protest movement,[4] also because the camps promoted spread of disease.[5] It also soured post-war relations between the two white 'tribes' of South Africa. The latter made it easier to forget that the blacks were also victims of the system.[6] France also established concentration camps in the 1930s, even calling them 'concentration camps', initially intended for refugees from the Spanish civil war.[7]

3.1   Nazi concentration camps

As mentioned above, concentration camps have become intimately connected in the public mind with Nazism and the Holocaust, known by the Jews as the *Shoah*, that is, 'the catastrophe.'

This is only half-justified, as the Nazis also used other methods to implement their infamous exterminatory scheme. More than a million Jews were thus killed by less 'industrial' methods than the gas chambers, for example, shooting by the notorious *Einsatzgruppen*,[8] while other hundreds of thousands were worked or starved to death in other concentration camps. Moreover, even though they constituted the bulk of the victims, the Jews were not the only victims, as the concentration camps also hosted political prisoners such as the Communists, and other ethnic groups such as the Romas (as part of what the Romas today call the *Porrajmos*),[9] as well as sexual minorities such as homosexuals[10] and religious ones such as Jehovah's Witnesses.[11] Finally, as mentioned above,

DOI: 10.1057/9781137502797.0007

not all concentration camps were exclusively devoted to the *Endlösung der Judenfrage* (final solution to the Jewish question'), but some were 'ordinary' detention centres for political enemies. In fact, recent research has revealed a much larger number of concentration camps and similar facilities, both in Germany and in the occupied territories, than were previously assumed to have existed.[12] This also means that most ordinary Germans must have known about the existence of these concentration camps, and that a much larger part of the German population must have witnessed the brutal treatment of the inmates, if only because they encountered them as forced labourers in various public works.[13]

An exception to this general rule was the extermination (or 'death') camps, because they were located outside the *Reich* ('realm'), because their existence was kept secret and because of the all-pervasive use of misleading euphemisms for their functions, referring to *Sonderbehandlung* ('special treatment') instead of mass murder. They also represent a small statistical minority of the camps, albeit generally by far the largest and those with (also by far) the most massive death toll of all. Some have attempted a typology of the camps (see Table 3.1),[14] but all such classifications should be taken cum grano salis. Not only was the Nazi regime

TABLE 3.1   *Main concentration camps in Nazi Germany and annexed/occupied territories*

Detention camps	Labour/miscellaneous official KZ camps	Combined labour and extermination camps	Extermination camps
Bergen-Belsen	Dachau	Mazjdanek	*Aktion Reinhart*
	Sachsenhausen	Auschwitz (I)[a]	*Camps* Chelmno
	Ravensbrück		Belzec
'Show-off'/	Buchenwald		Sobibor
Transit Camps	Flossenburg		Treblinka[c]
Theresienstadt[b]	Neuengamme		Birkenau
	Gross-Rosen Natzweiler		('Auschwitz II')
	Mauthausen		
	Stutthof Dora/		
	Nordhausen		

[a] *Gutman and Berenbaum, Anatomy (n. 1).*
[b] *S. Friedländer (2007) Nazi Germany and the Jews. II: The Years of Extermination* (New York: HarperCollins), 356–359.
[c] *Ibid., 351–355.*

Source: Feig, Konnilyn G. *Hitler's Death Camps: The Sanity of Madness* (New York: Holmes & Meier Publishers, 1979), 26–27 and other works.

DOI: 10.1057/9781137502797.0007

in general much less of an 'orderly', totalitarian and hierarchical regime than commonly assumed, and much more a 'feudal mess' of divided authorities, but the plans and rationales were also constantly changing,[15] which was also the case of the most notorious of them all, Auschwitz, which has come to symbolise the Holocaust.[16]

As mentioned above, the functions of the various camps were constantly changing, inter alia because of the conflicting demands of, on the one side, killing as many Jews as possible and, on the other side, winning (or, at least, not losing) the war. The most astounding fact was probably that the 'judeocide', almost to the very end, continued to take precedence over war efforts, for example, regarding the allocation of rail capacity. In the words of Hannah Arendt, writing in 1950:

> [I]t is not only the non-utilitarian character of the camps themselves; the senselessness of 'punishing' completely innocent people, the failure to keep them in a condition so that profitable work might be extorted from them, the superfluousness of frightening a completely subdued population, which gives them their distinctive and disturbing qualities, but their anti-utilitarian function, the fact that not even the supreme emergencies of military activities were allowed to interfere with these 'demographic policies.' It was as though the Nazis were convinced that it was of greater importance to run extermination factories than to win the war.[17]

Occasionally, however, the 'war-fighters' did gain the upper hand, producing a partial shift from 'death by gassing' to 'working to death' or even maximising the workload of the incarcerated Jews.[18] According to Wolfgang Sofsky, the fact that the concentration camp system was based on 'absolute power' made the labour system much worse than slavery and other forms of forced labour:

> [A]bsolute power transforms the significance of human labor. Labor in the camp should not be confused with forced labor. In forced labor, coercion is an instrument of work, but labor in the camp was a means of oppression, an instrument of terror. It was meant to humiliate, to torment, to break the power of the inmates to resist, to drain and destroy them. Anyone who employs forced laborers or slaves has a certain interest in preserving their physical strength. They are fed, clothed, and housed so as to be able to preserve their strength, to husband their energy. By contrast, labor in the camp sapped the life energy of the prisoners totally, irretrievably. The economy of the concentration camps was an economy of waste, the squandering of human labor power. (...) The prisoners did not work in order to produce. They labored in order to die.[19]

DOI: 10.1057/9781137502797.0007

That the slave labour was not economically rational does not mean that the Jews and their fellow inmates were not exploited to the utmost, down to posthumously having the gold fillings in their teeth extracted and their hair shaved off for industrial use (*sic!*).[20]

There were several proposals for a possible bombing of either the death camps or the railways connecting them to the rest of the world, but they were all rejected, also by the leaders of the Jewish community in Palestine (the *Yisuv*) such as Ben Gurion.[21] By late 1944, however it was obvious to most of the Nazi leadership (with the possible exception of Hitler himself) that defeat was near, which resulted in a replacement of the 'dead man working' with what we may call the 'dead man walking' paradigm, that is, the hurried evacuations of the camps (1944–1945) in front of the advancing allied (mainly Soviet) armies. This evacuation usually took the form of veritable 'death marches' reminiscent of those of the 1915 Armenian genocide in that the deaths from exhaustion and starvation en route were welcomed.[22]

The perpetrators of the Holocaust fall into several categories.[23] First of all, we have the SS *Totenkopfverbände* which, having displaced the SA ('*Sturmabteilung*'), were in charge of the entire camp system by the time the actual Holocaust took off, that is, from the early spring of 1942 until the end.[24] Just as Christopher Browning has shown about the members of the *Einsatzgruppen*, the vast majority of the SS personnel in the camps seem to have been 'ordinary men' (and women) as already hypothesised by Hannah Arendt *anno* 1950, and basically confirmed by subsequent research.[25] As far as the camp commanders and the upper echelons of the SS hierarchy were concerned, they were also a mixed bunch, only a minority of whom were ardent Jew-haters or sadists. Most of them were ordinary bureaucrats who saw themselves as cogs in a great wheel following orders from above, over the contents of which they had little or no influence. This may even have applied to the infamous commander of Auschwitz, Rudolf Höss (notorious for having 'killed more people than any man in history'),[26] the leading logistician of the Holocaust, Adolf Eichmann and his associates,[27] and the notorious commandant of first the Sobibor and then the Treblinka extermination camps, *Hauptsturmführer* Franz Stangl. When the latter was asked the question 'If they are going to kill them anyway, what was the point of all the humiliation, why the cruelty?' he seems to have seen himself as being primarily responsible for the well-being of his SS subalterns, charged with the dirty and profoundly unpleasant 'job' of mass murder, when he gave his oft-quoted answer, 'To

DOI: 10.1057/9781137502797.0007

condition those who actually had to carry out the policies – to make it possible for them to do what they did.'[28]

Another category was the SS doctors working in the camps, who have been studied extensively, for example, by the American psychiatrist Robert J. Lifton.[29] Even though their main task was 'selection at the ramp,' that is, the sorting of the Jews (and occasionally others) arriving by train into two main categories: those who would be put to work and those who went straight to the gas chambers. Most of these doctors had to cope with the obvious 'healing-killing paradox,' that is, the challenge of reconciling the Hippocratic oath obliging doctors to cure the sick and saving lives with the SS oath to the *Führer*, obliging them to kill on his command. This conundrum was solved by 'doubling,' that is, by creating another self:

> The Nazi doctors' immersion in the killing-healing paradox was crucial in setting the tone for doubling, as the Auschwitz self had to live by that paradox. To the extent that one embraces the far reaches of the Nazi vision of killing Jews in order to heal the Nordic race, the paradox disappears. The Auschwitz self can see itself as living out a commendable principle of 'racial hygiene' and working towards a noble vision of organic renewal: the creation of a vast 'German biotic community.'[30]

Even the most notorious of all the Nazi doctors, Josef Mengele, was apparently neither a sadist nor a particularly fanatic anti-Semite, which does not exculpate him.[31]

Besides the personnel in the camps, there were also the architects who had designed the camps, the engineers who developed, inter alia, the ovens for the crematoria, the chemists who invented the Zyklon-B gas (originally as a pesticide), those who discovered its utility for murdering Jews, and the firms that produced it,[32] as well as the staff of the euthanasia programme which predated the Holocaust, but provided many of the procedures and methods and some of the staff for the industrialised killing in the death camps.[33]

There is, for obvious reasons, not much to say about life in the death camps because of its extreme shortness, but in the other concentration camps (including the mixed extermination-labour camps) there was more of a camp life, albeit an incredibly miserable one.[34] According to the aforementioned excellent work by Sofsky, both space and time in the concentration camps were structured in a way supporting the absolute power of the regime, for example, by the deliberate and extreme humiliation and dehumanisation of the inmates.[35] Space, that is, the architecture

DOI: 10.1057/9781137502797.0007

was used to reflect and ipso facto cement the camp hierarchy, with separate quarters for the various categories of guards and administrators, the auxiliary staff recruited from among the inmates and the various groups belonging to the latter category. Time was, likewise, used to reflect absolute power. On the one hand, the guards deliberately abused the inmates' time with endless waiting (i.e., for name-calls) outside in the cold; but on the other hand they all along made it clear that all time was 'borrowed time' as anybody (both individually and as members of a group) could on extremely short notice and for no particular reason be shot or sent off to one of the death factories further east, thus making life completely precarious and unpredictable.

There was a camp hierarchy which, perversely, to a large extent mirrored that of the Nazi regime as such – even though this was a spurious relationship, concealing the basic fact that the politicals and criminals had longer life expectancies than Jews, and the young longer than the elderly.[36] There was also an economic system inside the camps, where inmates bartered just about everything.[37] Just as was the case for the ghettos (*vide infra*) the Nazis relied to a large extent on self-management in the camps, for example, by the appointment of the notorious *Kapos* ('prisoner functionary') and by the election of 'camp elders.'[38] Primo Levi lumped all these together as the category of the '*Prominenten*,' who were among 'the saved' as opposed to 'the drowned,' but ranging from the *Lagerältester* ('camp elder') at the top to the *Scheißminister* ('shit minister') and *Bademeister* ('bathing master') at the bottom of the hierarchy of the prominenten. Although exhibiting a certain empathy with the predicament that drove them to seek 'prominence,' Levi nevertheless described them as 'monsters of a sociality and insensitivity' with 'a capacity for hatred, unfulfilled in the direction of the oppressors, [which] will double back, beyond all reason, on the oppressed.'[39] At the very bottom of the hierarchy of victims were the '*Muselmänner*' described by Levi,

> Their life is short, but their number is endless; they, the *Muselmänner*, the drowned, form the backbone of the camp, an anonymous mass, continuously renewed and always identical, of non-men who march and labour in silence, the divine spark in them already too empty to really suffer. One hesitates to call them living: one hesitates to call their death death, in the face of which they have no fear, as they are too tired to understand.[40]

The fate of these 'living dead' was only marginally worse and more humiliating than the rest of the ordinary Jewish inmates, whose fate Levi described in his rightly celebrated autobiographical account, *If This Is a Man*.[41]

DOI: 10.1057/9781137502797.0007

3.2   The functional equivalent: Jewish ghettos

The word 'ghetto' was initially used about the special part of the city of Venice to which the Jews were confined,[42] not only because of a government decision, but also because of a long and partly self-chosen habit of segregation. In Eastern Europe, however, there was a much more malign background, both of pogroms[43] which made moving together seem the safest policy for Jews, and deliberate state policies of keeping them segregated from the rest of the society.

The latter was initially also the policy of the Nazi regime in Germany. Addressing a small audience of devout Nazis, Adolf Hitler in 1935 thus explained his vision for the Jews as 'Out of all the professions, into a ghetto, enclosed in a territory where they can behave as becomes their nature, while the German people look on as one looks at wild animals.'[44] True to his erratic style, however, three years later, Hitler turned down Hermann Göring's proposal to establish regular ghettos, siding with Reinhard Heydrich who opposed this.[45] While the ghettoisation of Jews in Germany (including, following the *Anschluß* in 1938, Austria) never really got anywhere, it became a central companion of the German eastwards expansion which, ironically, brought much larger Jewish populations under German control. When German Jews were deported to Poland and other occupied and/or annexed countries, they were, along with the indigenous Jews, pushed into ghettos,[46] albeit, as it should soon become obvious, mainly intended as half-way stations to the aforementioned death camps.

Within these spaces of confinement, the Nazi masters were quite skilful in enrolling members of the victim population in the administration, thus saving increasingly scarce manpower. Just as they used Kapos in the concentration camps (*vide supra*), they delegated similar tasks in the ghettos to so-called 'Jewish Councils' (*Judenräte*),[47] playing on a special, and profoundly perverted, form of rationality, as explained by Zygmunt Bauman in his rightly acclaimed work on *Modernity and the Holocaust*:

> To sacrifice some in order to save many, this was the most frequent and recurring refrain in the recorded apologias of the *Judenräte* leaders (...) If they had a choice, none of the Jewish councillors or policemen would board the train of self-destruction. But they did not have that choice (...). What the experience of the Holocaust revealed in all its awesome consequences was a distinction between the rationality of the actor (a psychological phenomenon) and

DOI: 10.1057/9781137502797.0007

the rationality of the action (measured by its objective consequences for the actor).[48]

Although some of the chairmen of the councils behaved abominably, others took a utilitarian approach to the intolerable dilemmas, as did the vilified chairman of the Łódź ghetto, Mordechai Chaim Rumkowski, who in a speech of 4 September 1942 explained his 'strategy' faced with the request to select 20,000 Jews for 'deportation,' by that time well-known as a euphemism for certain death in the death camps:

> [D]espite the horrible responsibility, we have to accept the evil order. I have to perform this bloody operation myself. I simply must cut off limbs to save the body! I have to take away the children, because otherwise others will also be taken (...) With all my might, I strove to repeal this evil order. And as it has been impossible to rescind it, I have tried to make it milder. Only yesterday, I ordered the registration of children nine years of age, because I have endeavored to save children of at least this single age group, from nine to ten. But they did not relent, and I have succeeded only in saving the ten-years-old. (...) Deliver to me those sick ones and it may be possible to save the healthy ones instead. (...) [I]n times of disaster one has to weigh and measure, who can and should be saved. To my mind those are to be spared in the first place who have any chance of survival, not those who cannot survive anyway.[49]

The chairman of the largest of all the ghettos, Adam Czerniakow of the Warsaw ghetto managed to secure himself a more honourable place in history than Rumkowski by committing suicide, faced with the order to select orphans for 'deportation.'[50] There was generally very little active resistance by the Jewish residents of the ghettos – and, in fact, very small prospects of achieving anything by resistance – but there were some instances of heroic resistance,[51] with the Warsaw ghetto uprising as the epitome.[52]

Unfortunately for genocide studies because of the propensity for obfuscation, the term 'ghetto' is today almost exclusively applied to what is in fact a very different phenomenon, that is, parts of modern cities where national or ethnic minorities tend to cluster and where social problems and crime tend to flourish, regardless of whether there is any form of fencing in, which is quite rare.[53] These 'ghettos' might thus best be conceptualised as the 'ugly twin' of the aforementioned 'gated communities,' in which the privileged and affluent seek protection against their less fortunate fellow countrymen.

DOI: 10.1057/9781137502797.0007

3.3   Post-WWII concentration camps (?)

The distinctions between concentration camps and prison camps (*vide supra*) or prisoner-of-war camps (*vide infra*) are far from clear, and the fact that nobody wants to bring to mind the horrors of Auschwitz with themselves cast as *genocidaires* means that the term is almost never used by those who establish camps which might in fact deserve the concentration camp label. On the other hand, their critics may use the label too frivolously in their attempts to vilify their adversaries. These factors make it harder to identify and verify the existence of concentration camps. There are, however, some fairly obvious candidates.

In their struggle against the Mau-Mau insurgents in colonial Kenya in the early 1950s, the British resorted, among many other means of counter-insurgency such as hangings and 'hearts and minds operations,' to the large-scale encampment of the fighters as well as suspected supporters. This policy has been likened to the Soviet Gulag, but the term 'concentration camps' may in fact be a more befitting label, as quite a lot of the incarcerated Kenyans (mainly Kikuyus) were civilians who had not been convicted of anything.[54]

During the wars in the wake of the Yugoslav disintegration, a lot of attention was paid to what was sometimes described as concentration camps. In particular one image, that of a Bosnian Muslim prisoner at the Trnopolje camp, Ficret Alic, whose emaciated state brought to mind the aforementioned *Muselmänner*, had an immense effect. Even though quite convincing cases have later been made that this particular photo was a forgery,[55] there is no doubt that the Serbs maintained camps for the incarceration of their prisoners, which might well deserve the label 'concentration camps,' even though it evidently overshoots the mark to call them 'death camps' or even 'extermination camps.' On the question of possible forgery, the present author is in no position to assess the contrasting claims and maintains the position of an agnostic. On the other hand, the Bosnian Serbs stand accused of inventing another and especially nasty variety of (concentration) camps, namely so-called 'rape camps.'[56] If there is any truth in the allegations (as seems likely) they were probably established as a means of a planned genocide, mainly targeted at the Muslims (also, somewhat misleadingly, known as 'Bosniaks') as a group whose ethno-religious identity could be destroyed, at least as far as the next generation was concerned, by having its female members forcefully impregnated by Serbian men.[57]

DOI: 10.1057/9781137502797.0007

These camps were certainly not the first concentration camps established in the former Yugoslavia. In the course of the World War II, the independent state of Croatia, established by the fascist *Ustaša* movement, aligned with Nazi Germany, had thus constructed a major camp complex called Jasenovac close to Zagreb where the *Ustaša* is estimated to have killed between 77,000 and 99,000 Serbs, Jews and Roma, in addition to which another approximately 200,000 people were murdered by other means, either in Croatia itself or in camps run by its German allies.[58]

3.4 Summary

As the above account of concentration camps has, hopefully, shown, they should have better be analysed as a genus with several species than as a single species in its own right. Not only were there many forms of concentration camps, ranging from places of detention to veritable factories of death with loci of forced labour somewhere in-between the two. Moreover, even though they proved chillingly effective as means of mass murder, the concentration camps of Nazi Germany (and some of its allies) were merely one tool in well-furnished 'tool-box' for mass murder alongside killing squads such as the notorious *Einsatzgruppen* with their 'hands-on' approach. What the Nazi camps of all types had in common was their factory-like organisation and the fact that a bewildering degree of self-management in which 'victims became killers'[59] – a feature they shared with another form of camps, namely the ghettos, particularly those established in Eastern Europe.

Notes

1   Y. Gutman and M. Berenbaum (1998) *Anatomy of the Auschwitz Death Camp* (Bloomington, IN: Indiana University Press).
2   K. Mühlhahn (2010) 'The Concentration Camp in Global Historical Perspective,' *History Compass*, 8:6, 543–561; I.R. Smith and A. Stucki (2011) 'The Colonial Development of Concentration Camps (1868–1902),' *Journal of Imperial and Commonwealth History*, 39:3, 417–437; J. Hyslop (2011) 'The Invention of the Concentration Camp: Cuba, Southern Africa and the Philippines,' *South African Historical Journal*, 63:2, 251–276; J.L. Tone (2006) *War and Genocide in Cuba, 1895–1898* (Chapel Hill, NC: University of North Carolina Press), 193–224; P.A. Kramer (2006) 'Race-Making and Colonial

DOI: 10.1057/9781137502797.0007

Violence in the U.S. Empire: The Philippine-American War as Race War,' *Diplomatic History*, 30:2, 169–210; R.E.Welch, Jr. (1974) 'American Atrocities in the Philippines: The Indictment and the Response,' *Pacific Historical Review*, 43:2, 233–253.

3   T. Pakenham (1992) *The Boer War* (London: Abacus), 493–517; L. Weiss (2011) 'Exceptional Space: Concentration Camps and Labor Compounds in Late Nineteenth-Century South Africa,' in G. Myers and A. Moshenka (eds.) *Archaeologies of Internment* (New York: Springer), 21–32; J. de Reuck (1999) 'Social Suffering and the Politics of Pain: Observations on the Concentration Camps in the Anglo-Boer War, 1899–1902,' *English in Africa*, 26:2, 69–88; E. van Heyningen (2009) 'The Concentration Camps of the South African (Anglo-Boer) War, 1900–1902,' *History Compass*, 7:1, 22–43.

4   P.M. Krebs (1992) "The Last of the Gentlemen's Wars': Women in the Boer War Concentration Camp Controversy,' *History Workshop*, 33, 38–56; M. Hasian Jr. (2003) 'The 'Hysterical" Emily Hobhouse and the Boer War Concentration Camp Controversy,' *Western Journal of Communication*, 67:2, 138–163.

5   E. van Heyningen (2010) 'A Tool for Modernisation? The Boer Concentration Camps of the South African War, 1900–1902,' *South African Journal of Science*, 106:5–6, 52–61.

6   S.V. Kessler (1999) 'The Black and Coloured Concentration Camps of the Anglo-Boer War, 1899–1902: Shifting the Paradigm from Sole Martyrdom to Mutual Suffering,' *Historia*, 44:1, 110–147.

7   D. Peschanski (2002) *La France des camps. L'internement 1938–1946* (Paris: Gallimard).

8   D. Stone (1999) 'Modernity and Violence: Theoretical Reflections on the *Einsatzgruppen*,' *Journal of Genocide Research*, 1:3, 367–378; Y. Büchler (1986) 'Kommandostab Reichsführer-SS: Himmler's Personal Murder Brigades in 1941,' *Holocaust and Genocide Studies*, 1:1, 11–25; C. Browning (2001) *Ordinary Men: Reserve Police Battalion 101 and the Final Slution in Poland* (London: Penguin Books); A. Angrick (2008) 'The Men of *Einsatsgruppe D*: An Inside View of a State-Sanctioned Killing Unit in the 'Third Reich",' in O. Jensen and C-C. W. Szejnmann (eds.) *Ordinary People as Mass Murderers: Perpetrators in Comparative Perspectives* (Houndmills: Palgrave Macmillan), 78–96.

9   G. Lewy: 'Gypsies and Jews under the Nazis,' *Holocaust and Genocide Studies*, 13:3, 383–404.

10 H. Heger (1994) *The Men with the Pink Triangle* (Boston, MA: Alyson Publishers).

11 G. Yonan (1999) 'Spiritual Resistance of Christian Conviction in Nazi Germany: The Case of Jehovah's Witnesses,' *Journal of Church and State*, 41:2, 307–322.

12 The Center for Advanced Holocaust Studies at the United States Holocaust Memorial Museum thus counts a total of 42,000 facilities (including

DOI: 10.1057/9781137502797.0007

ghettos), to which their planned seven-volume *Encyclopedia of Camps and Ghettos, 1933–1945* (under publication by the Indiana University Press) is devoted. See www.ushmm.org/ research/publications/encyclopedia-camps-ghettos.

13 K. Fings (2010) 'The Public Face of the Camps,' in J. Caplan and N. Wachsmann (eds.) *Concentration Camps in Nazi Germany* (London: Routledge), 108–126.

14 K.G. Feig (1979) *Hitler's Death Camps: The Sanity of Madness* (New York: Holmes and Meier), 26–27; E. Kogon (2006) *The Theory and Practice of Hell: The German Concentration Camps and the System behind Them.* 2nd ed. (New York: Farrar, Straus and Giroux); Caplan and Wachsmann (eds.) *Concentration Camps* (n. 13); W. Sofsky (1997) *The Order of Terror: The Concentration Camp* (Princeton, NJ: Princeton University Press); D. Dwork and R.J. van Pelt (2002) *Holocaust: A History* (New York: W.W. Norton), 284–315, 356–374.

15 N. Wachsmann (2010) 'The Dynamics of Destruction: The Development of Concentration Camps, 1933–1945,' in Caplan and Wachsmann (eds.) *Concentration Camps* (n. 13), 17–43.

16 R-J. van Pelt (1998) 'A Site in Search of a Mission,' in Gutman and Berenbaum, *Anatomy* (n. 1), 93–156.

17 H. Arendt (1950) 'Social Science Techniques and the Study of the Concentration Camp,' *Jewish Social Studies*, 12:1, 49–64.

18 J. Fear (2004) 'The Business of Genocide: The SS, Slave Labour and the Concentration Camps,' *Business History Review*, 78:1, 163–168. See also M. Spoerer and J. Fleischhacker (2002) 'Forced Laborers in Nazi Germany: Categories, Numbers and Survivors,' *Journal of Interdisciplinary History*, 33:2, 169–204; J.C. Wagner (2010) 'Work and Extermination in the Concentration Camps,' in Caplan and Wachsmann (eds.) *Concentration Camps* (n. 13), 127–148.

19 Sofsky, *Order of Terror* (n. 14), 21–22, 167–195.

20 F. Piper (1998) 'The System of Prisoner Exploitation,' in Gutman and Berenbaum, *Anatomy* (n. 1), 34–49; A. Strzelecki (1998) 'The Plunder of Victims and Their Corpses,' ibid., 246–266.

21 D.S. Wyman (1998) 'Why Auschwitz Wasn't Bombed,' in Gutman and Berenbaum, *Anatomy* (n. 128), 569–587; S.G. Erdheim (1997) 'Could the Allies Have Bombed Auschwitz-Birkenau?' *Holocaust and Genocide Studies*, 7:2, 129–170.

22 D. Blatman (2010) 'The Death Marches and the Final Phase of Nazi Genocide,' in Caplan and Wachsmann (eds.) *Concentration Camps* (n. 13), 167–185; D.J. Goldhagen (2010) *Worse than War: Genocide, Eliminationism, and the Ongoing Assault on Humanity* (London: Little, Brown), 104–110.

23 For an excellent typology see R. Hilberg (1993) *Perpetrators, Victims, Bystanders: The Jewish Catastrope 1933–1945* (New York: Harper Perennial);

DOI: 10.1057/9781137502797.0007

See also K. Ohrt (2010) 'The Concentration Camp Personnel,' in Caplan and Wachsmann (eds.) *Concentration Camps* (n. 13), 44–57.

24   R. Koehl (1962) 'The Character of the Nazi SS,' *Journal of Modern History*, 34:3, 275–283; L. Alexander (1948) 'War Crimes and Their Motivation: The Socio-Psychological Structure of the SS and the Criminalization of a Society,' *Journal of Criminal Law and Criminology*, 39:3, 298–326; Sofsky, *Order of Terror* (n. 1), 97–116; A. Lasik (1998) 'Historical-Sociological Profile of the Nazi SS,' in Gutman and Berenbaum, *Anatomy* (n. 1), 271–287.

25   Arendt, 'Social Science Techniques' (n. 17); M. Mann (2005) *The Dark Side of Democracy: Explaining Ethnic Cleansing* (Cambridge: Cambridge University Press), 212–278; C-C. W. Szejnmann (2008) 'Perpetrators of the Holocaust: A Historiography,' in Jensen and Szejnmann, *Ordinary People* (n. 8), 25–54; H. Irmtraud (2008) 'Female Concentration Camp Guards: Three Case Studies,' ibid., 120–142.

26   J. Tenenbaum (1953) 'Auschwitz in Retrospect: The Self-Portrait of Rudolf Hoess, Commander of Auschwitz,' *Jewish Social Studies*, 15:3–4, 203–236, quote from p. 203; A. Lasik (1998) 'Rudolf Höss: Manager of Crime,' in Gutman and Berenbaum, *Anatomy* (n. 1), 288–300.

27   H. Arendt (2006) *Eichmann in Jerusalem: A Report on the Banality of Evil* (London: Penguin); H. Saferian (2010) *Eichmann's Men* (Cambridge: Cambridge University Press).

28   E. Staub (1989) *The Roots of Evil: The Origins of Genocide and Other Group Violence* (Cambridge: Cambridge University Press), 137.

29   R.J. Lifton (1986) *The Nazi Doctors: Medical Killing and the Psychology of Genocide* (New York: Basic Books).

30   Ibid., 430–431.

31   Z. Zofka (1986) 'Der KZ-Arzt Joseph Mengele. Zur Typologies eines NS-Verbrecher,' *Vierteljahresschrifte für Zeitgeschichte*, 34:2, 245–267; M.A. Grodin et al. (2011) 'The Trial that Never Happened: Josef Mengele and the Twins of Auschwitz,' *War Crimes, Genocide and Crimes against Humanity*, 5, 3–89; H. Kubica (1998) 'The Crimes of Josef Mengele,' in Gutman and Berenbaum, *Anatomy* (n. 128), 317–337.

32   C.R. Browning (2005) *The Origins of the Final Solution: The Evolution of Nazi Jewish Policy, 1939–1942* (London: Arrow Books), 352–373; A. van Baar and W. Huisman (2012) 'The Oven Builders of the Holocaust: A Case Study of Corporate Complicity in International Crimes,' *British Journal of Criminology*, 52:6, 1033–1050; F. Piper (1998) 'Gas Chambers and Crematoria,' in Gutman and Berenbaum, *Anatomy* (n. 1), 157–182; J-C. Pressac and R-J. van Pelt (1998) 'The Machinery of Mass Murder at Auschwitz,' ibid. 183–245; S. Friedländer (2007), *Nazi Germany and the Jews. II The Years of Extermination* (New York: Harper Collins), 458–459, 503–504.

DOI: 10.1057/9781137502797.0007

33 M. Beer (1987) 'Die Entwicklung der Gaswagen beim Mord an den Juden,' *Vierteljahreshefte für Zeitgeschichte*, 35:3, 403–417.

34 F. Pingel (2010) 'Social Life in an Unsocial Environment: The Inmates' Struggle for Survival,' in Caplan and Wachsmann (eds.) *Concentration Camps* (n. 13), 58–81.

35 Sofsky, *Order of Terror* (n. 14), 47–93.

36 Ibid., 117–129.

37 A. Myers (2011) 'The Things of Auschwitz,' in A. Myers and G. Moshenka, eds., Archaeologies of Internment (New York: Springer), 75–88.

38 Sofsky, *Order of Terror* (n. 14), 130–152; H.G. Adler (1960) 'Selbstverwaltung und Widerstand in den Konzentrationslagern der SS,' *Vierteljahresschrifte für Zeitgeschichte*, 8:3, 221–236; Kogon, *The Theory and Practice of Hell* (n. 14), 51–59; D. Czech (1998) 'The Auschwitz Prisoner Administration,' in Gutman and Berenbaum, *Anatomy* (n. 1), 363–378; R. Wolf (2007) 'Judgement in the Grey Zone: The Third Auschwitz (Kapo) Trial in Frankfurt 1968,' *Journal of Genocide Research*, 9:4, 617–635; O. Ben-Naftali and Y. Tuval (2006) 'Punishing International Crimes Committed by the Persecuted: The Kapo Trials in Israel (1950s–1960s),' *Journal of International Criminal Justice*, 4:1, 128–178.

39 P. Levi (1987) 'If This Is a Man,' in idem. *If This Is a Man and The Truce* (London: Abacus), 96–97.

40 Sofsky, *Order of Terror* (n. 14), 199–205; G. Agamben (1998) *Homo Sacer: Sovereign Power and Bare Life* (Stanford, CA: Stanford University Press), 103–104; idem (2002) *Remnants of Auschwitz: The Witness and the Archive* (New York: Zone Books, 2002), 41–86; L. Skitolsky (2012) 'Tracing Theory of the Body of the 'Walking Dead': Der Muselmann and the Course of Holocaust Studies,' *Shofar*, 30:2, 74–90.

41 Levi, *If This Is a Man* (n. 39), 17.

42 D. Michman (2011) *The Emergence of Jewish Ghettos During the Holocaust* (Cambridge: Cambridge University Press), 20–24; S. Debenedetti-Stow (1992) 'The Etymology of 'Ghetto': New Evidence from Rome,' *Jewish History*, 6:1–2 (1992), 79–85; B. Ravid (1987) 'The Legal Status of the Jews in Venice to 1509,' *Proceedings of the American Academy of Jewish Research*, 54, 169–202; D. Calabi and M-P. Gaviano (1997) 'Les quartiers juifs en Italie entre 15e et 17e siècle. Quelques hypothèses de travail,' *Annales*, 52:4, 777–797.

43 The very first recorded pogrom seems to have taken place in AD 38. See P.W. van der Horst (2003) *Philo's Flaccus: The First Pogrom* (Leiden: Brill, 2003), passim.

44 Quote from S. Friedländer (1998) *Nazi Germany and the Jews. I: The Years of Persecution, 1933-1939* (New York: HarperCollins), 143.

45 Ibid., 283.

DOI: 10.1057/9781137502797.0007

46 Friedländer, *Nazi Germany and the Jews. II* (n. 32), 38–39, 61–63, 104–108,
144–160, 241–247, 310–318, 322–323, 387–395, 433–438, 531–532, 584–586; C.M.
Lewin (2002) 'Ghettos in the Holocaust: The Improvisation of Social Order
in a Culture of Terror', in C.J. Greenhouse et al. (eds.) *Ethnography in Unstable
Places: Everyday Lives in Contexts of Dramatic Political Change* (Durham, NC:
Duke University Press), 37–60.

47 I. Trunk (1996) *Judenrat: The Jewish Councils in Eastern Europe under Nazi
Occupation.* 2nd ed. (Lincoln, NE: University of Nebraska Press); Arendt,
Eichmann (n. 27), 117–125, 169–170, 196; Hilberg, *Perpetrators* (n. 23), 105–117;
Center for Advanced Holocaust Studies (2005) *Ghettos 1939–1945: New
Research and Perspectives on Definition, Daily Life and Survival. Symposion
Presentations* (Washington, DC: United States Holocaust Memorial Museum).

48 Z. Bauman (2000) *Modernity and the Holocaust.* 2nd ed. (Cambridge: Polity
Press), 140, 149.

49 Quoted in Trunk, *Judenrat* (n. 47), 423.

50 R. Hilberg et al., eds. (1999) *The Warsaw Diary of Adam Czerniakow: Prelude to
Doom* (Chicago, IL: Ivan R. Dee Publisher).

51 D.B. Kopel (2007) 'Armed Resistance to the Holocaust', *Journal of Firearms
and Public Policy*, 19, 144–162; R. Suhl, ed. (1967) *They Fought Back* (New
York: Paperback Library); N. Tec (1997) *Jewish Resistance: Facts, Omissions,
Distortions* (Washington, DC: United States Holocaust Museum).
Trunk, *Judenrat* (n. 177); B. Klein (1960) 'The Judenrat', *Jewish Social Studies*,
22:1, 27–42; F. Fox (1995) 'The Jewish Ghetto Police: Some Reflexions', *East
European Jewish Affairs*, 25:2, 41–47.

52 Friedländer, *Nazi Germany and the Jews. II* (n. 32), 524–529; M. Arens (2005)
'The Jewish Military Organization (ZZW) in the Warsaw Ghetto', *Holocaust
and Genocide Studies*, 19:2, 201–225; R.L. Einwohner (2010) 'Leadership,
Authority, and Collective Action: Jewish Resistance in the Ghettos of Warsaw
and Vilna', *American Behavioralist Scientist*, 50:10, 1306–1326; idem (2009) 'The
Need to Know: Cultured Ignorance and Jewish Resistance in the Ghettos of
Warsaw, Vilna and Łódź', *Sociological Quarterly*, 50:3, 407–430.

53 J. Flint (2009) 'Cultures, Ghettos and Camps: Sites of Exception and
Antagonism in the City', *Housing Studies*, 24:4, 417–431.

54 C. Elkins (2005) *Imperial Reckoning: The Untold Story of Britain's Gulag in Kenya*
(New York: Henry Holt), 120–191; D. Anderson (2005) *Histories of the Hanged:
The Dirty War in Kenya and the End of Empire* (New York: W.W. Norton),
311–327; A.R. Baggallay (2011) 'Myths of Mau Mau Expanded: Rehabilitation
in Kenya's Detention Camps, 1954–60', *Journal of Eastern African Studies*, 5:3,
553–578.

55 L.J. Kalinich (2000) 'Beyond Horror: Sensationalism and the Hermeneutics
of War', *Journal of the North American Society for Serbian Studies*, 14:2, 143–158;
D. Campbell (2002) 'Atrocity, Memory, Photography: Imagining the

DOI: 10.1057/9781137502797.0007

Concentration Camps of Bosnia: The Case of ITN versus Living Marxism,' 1–2, *Journal of Human Rights*, 1:1, 1–33 and 1:2, 143–172; D. Johnstone (2002) *Fools' Crusade: Yugoslavia, NATO and Western Delusions* (London: Pluto Press), 68–90. For counter-arguments see M.A. Hoare (2003) 'Genocide in the Former Yugoslavia: A Critique of Left Revisionism's Denial,' *Journal of Genocide Research*, 5:4, 543–563.

56 T.A. Salzman (1998) 'Rape Camps as a Means of Ethnic Cleansing: Religious, Cultural, and Ethical Responses to Rape Victims in the Former Yugoslavia,' *Human Rights Quarterly*, 20:2, 348–378; N.M. Naimark (2001) *Fires of Hatred: Ethnic Cleansing in Twentieth-Century Europe* (Cambridge, MA: Harvard University Press), 160–161, 167–170; L. Sharlach (2009) 'State Rape: Sexual Violence as Genocide,' in S. Totten and P.R. Bartrop (eds.) *The Genocide Studies Reader* (London: Routledge), 180–192, especially 184–186; A. Jones (2011), *Genodice: A Comprehensive Introduction*, 2nd ed. (London: Routledge), 322–324; E.D. Weitz (2003) *A Century of Genocide: Utopias of Race and Nation* (Princeton, NJ: Princeton University Press), 227–228; K.E. Smith (2010) *Genocide and the Europeans* (Cambridge: Cambridge University Press), 110–112, 118–119; R.M. Hayden (2008) 'Mass Killings and Images of Genocide in Bosnia, 1941–5 and 1992–5,' in D. Stone (ed.) *The Historiography of Genocide* (Houndmills, Basingstoke: Palgrave Macmillan), 487–516, especially 498–502.

57 S.K. Fisher (1996) 'Occupation of the Womb: Forced Impregnation as Genocide,' *Duke Law Journal*, 46:1, 91–133; C. Card (2008) 'The Paradox of Genocidal Rape Aimed at Enforced Pregnancy,' *Southern Journal of Philosophy*, 46, 176–189.

58 L. Boban (1990) 'Jasenovac and the Manipulation of History,' *East European Politics and Society*, 4:3, 580–592; D. Reinhartz (1999) 'Unmarked Graves: The Destruction of the Yugoslav Roma in the Balkan Holocaust, 1941–1945,' *Journal of Genocide Research*, 1:1, 81–89; A. Korb (2010) 'Understanding Ustaša Violence,' ibid., 12:1–2, 1–18; D. Mirkovic (2000) 'The Historic Link between the Ustasha Genocide and the Croato-Serb Civil War, 1991–1995,' ibid., 2:3, 363–373.

59 M. Mamdani (2001) *When Victims Become Killers: Colonialism, Nativism, and the Genocide in Rwanda* (Oxford: James Currey).

DOI: 10.1057/9781137502797.0007

4
Camps for/in War

Abstract: *Camps play important roles in wars, one being detention of prisoners-of-war whose status is regulated in international humanitarian law. Insurgents and rebels also tend to establish training camps, typically in neighbouring countries. Camp-like facilities such as 'strategic hamlets' are also a central element in counter-insurgency warfare, intended to separate the guerrillas from the peasantry, but such arrangements may also be used for social engineering, for example, collectivisation and other attempts to 'capture' the 'uncaptured peasantry'.*

Keywords: counter-insurgency; guerrillas; humanitarian law; POW; prisoners-of-war; Red Cross; strategic hamlets; training camps; terrorists; uncaptured peasantry

Møller, Bjørn. *Refugees, Prisoners and Camps: A Functional Analysis of the Phenomenon of Encampment.* Basingstoke: Palgrave Macmillan, 2015. DOI: 10.1057/9781137502797.0008.

DOI: 10.1057/9781137502797.0008

Just as war provides an almost ideal setting for genocide and other forms as mass atrocities,[1] it also tends to create a need for various forms of camps which therefore tend to proliferate in times of war. Besides making masses of people flee, thus creating a need for camps to accommodate both internally displaced persons (IDPs) and refugees, to which the next chapter is devoted, war also creates a need for other forms of camps which are even more directly related to the war itself. In this chapter we shall take a closer view at some of these camp categories.

4.1 Prisoners-of-war camps

Prisoners-of-war (POWs) are special in several respects.[2] First of all, their rights and obligations have long been formalised in the laws of war, usually referred to as international humanitarian law (IHL), the main conventions and protocols of which are listed in Table 4.1.[3]

Even before this rather extensive codification of norms, there were fairly consensual, albeit unwritten, norms pertaining to combatants who surrendered or were captured in wars, at least within (what was regarded as) the 'civilised world' and protecting mainly other 'civilised' peoples.[4] Gradually such norms came to constitute one part of a whole body of 'just war' (*bellum justum*) theory,[5] initially mainly produced by catholic theologians

TABLE 4.1 *International treaties and conventions on the treatment of prisoners-of-war*

Year	Name
1863	Resolution establishing the Red Cross
1864	Geneva Convention on the Treatment of Wounded
1906	Geneva Convention on the Wounded and Sick
1929	Geneva Convention on the Wounded and Sick Geneva Convention on Prisoners-of-War
1949	Geneva Conventions I Amelioration of the Condition of the Wounded and Sick in Armed Forces in the Field II Amelioration of the Condition of Wounded, Sick and Shipwrecked Members of Armed Forces at Sea III Treatment of Prisoners of War
1977	Additional Protocols to the 1949 Geneva Conventions I Relating to the Protection of Victims of International Armed Conflicts II Protection of Victims of Non-International Armed Conflicts

Source: ICRC's database Treaties and States Parties to Such Treaties at www.icrc.org/ihl.

DOI: 10.1057/9781137502797.0008

from St. Augustin to St. Bonaventura and St. Thomas Aquinas,[6] but gradually extended to the secular realm, and with counterparts in Protestantism and other religions.[7] Most of what today is subsumed under the rubric of IHL was thus formerly viewed as *jus in bello* provisions, regulating the waging of war for both those complying with the *jus ad bellum* (the right to go to war, mainly referring to self-defence) provisions and those who, qua aggressors, were in violation of these provisions.[8] Arguably at least part of the body of IHL treaties and conventions also represents customary law, binding also non-signatories as *jus cogens* ('compelling law').[9]

Another component of what we may justifiably call the 'IHL regime' is an international organisation serving as custodian and implementer, in which role we find the International Committee of the Red Cross (ICRC), which was founded in 1863[10] and today has national chapters (Red Cross societies) in virtually all countries of the world, in Muslim ones called the Red Crescent societies.[11] Even though ICRC has assumed other tasks, initially the POW problematic was its only task, and it has remained one of the most central ones.

Considering that taking enemy soldiers captive and providing for them is much more cumbersome and expensive than simply killing captives (especially during, but also after a war), both the very establishment and remarkable resilience of this 'POW regime' seems to call for an explanation. Two factors may be important in this respect. First of all, soldiers (and, even more so, officers) have an obvious interests in protection against being killed and a guarantee of decent treatment, as everybody risks, and is surely concerned about, ending up as a POW – especially considering that soldiering and the commanding of troops was very much an international profession, meaning that the same officers might well be on different sides in different wars, or even different stages of the same war. Second, each side in most conflicts have always understood that the bulk of the troops and officers of the respective other side were not to be blamed for the war, but were simply doing their job or performing their national (or other) duty in killing or trying to kill enemy troops. As long as they did so, they were legitimate targets, but as soon as they were *hors de combat* (as a result of surrender, capture or injury) they ceased being so, and should be treated as colleagues endowed with certain rights and entitled to benefits commensurable with their ranks. This norm was already very eloquently articulated by Rousseau in his *Social Contract*:

> War then is a relation, not between man and man, but between State and State, and individuals are enemies only accidentally, not as men, nor even as

DOI: 10.1057/9781137502797.0008

citizens,' but as soldiers; not as members of their country, but as its defenders
(...). The object of the war being the destruction of the hostile State, the other
side has a right to kill its defenders, while they are bearing arms; but as soon
as they lay them down and surrender, they cease to be enemies or instruments of the enemy, and become once more merely men, whose life no one
has any right to take.[12]

In line with this, the ICRC is usually allowed to operate as long as it
complies with its own rules, the most important of which is to remain
independent, neutral and impartial. This is, alas, becoming increasingly
difficult as 'war' is rapidly evolving from an international to a predominantly intra-state problem accompanied by a blurring of distinctions
between combatants and civilians.[13]

The existence of POW camps does, however, predate the founding of
the ICRC. Perhaps the first dedicated POW camp was thus established at
Norman Cross, UK, in 1797 after the war against revolutionary France,
but it was subsequently also used to accommodate the POWs 'produced'
by the Napoleonic Wars.[14] The POW camps of the American Civil War
were special because the inmates belonged to the same nation, but they
were nevertheless (almost) regular soldiers and generally treated as
such.[15]

As wars became more 'total' in the twentieth century with the World
Wars I and II as the epitomes, not only did the numbers of POWs
reach staggering proportions, but violations of the conventions also
seem to have become not only more frequent and severe, but occasionally also more deliberate.[16] In World War II (WWII) it also seems to
have taken considerably more than 'mere defeat' to make combatants
surrender, perhaps as a result of the high ideological stakes in this war,
perhaps for fear of vengeance, which was arguably counter-productive
for the winning side which therefore did little to lure enemy troops to
surrender.[17]

During WWII a mind-boggling 3.5 million Soviet POWs thus seem
to have been deliberately starved to death by the *Wehrmacht* (Defence
Force) in their POW camps.[18] However, while this may simply be what
was to be expected by one of history's most evil regimes, it is perhaps
more discomforting that virtually all of the victorious powers seem to
have mistreated German POWs in violation of their obligations under
the aforementioned conventions.[19] There were significant differences,
however, as the Western allies at least kept the mortality rate among their
German POWs quite low, whereas the rates of the USSR and Yugoslavia

DOI: 10.1057/9781137502797.0008

were of almost 'genocidal' proportions, that is, 35.8 and 41.2 per cent, respectively, which is the main reason for the aggregate mortality rate of 10.9 per cent of more than 11 million German POWs.[20] In most cases, the very large numbers of POWs in camps was quite a heavy burden on those obliged to cater for the captured enemy soldiers, which explains why they were in most cases used for compulsory labour.[21] In other cases they were simply killed, the best-known example of which may be the deliberate killing of POWs perpetrated by the Red Army against Polish officers in the Katyn Forest.[22]

More recently two IHL lacunae have attracted considerable attention, that is, terrorists and contractors. As far as the former are concerned, in the wake of the terrorist attacks of 11 September 2001 ('9/11' for short), the United States declared a 'War on Terror(ism).' While one would have expected that this label would have entitled the suspected terrorists captured in the course of this 'war' to treatment as POWs, the US has obstinately until the present day denied them this status. In an attempt to justify this, the Bush administration invented a new term for this category, namely 'unlawful combatants' to whom neither criminal law with its habeas corpus and other norms nor IHL allegedly applied.[23] The US government even went out of its way to establish a legal no-man's land beyond both national and international jurisdiction by selecting as its main detention facility the American base at Guantanamo Bay in Cuba, nicknamed Camp X-ray (*vide supra*).[24] Even though the new administration of Barack Obama promised to eliminate this foucauldian heterotopia, virtually nothing had by the time of writing been accomplished.[25]

The other lacuna hosts the so-called 'contractors,'[26] including the personnel of private military companies (PMCs), of the services of whom many states increasingly avail themselves,[27] again following the lead of the US, for example, in its military intervention in and subsequent occupation of Iraq.[28] The Geneva Conventions *expressis verbis* exclude mercenaries from the norms applying to combatants. Article 47 in the Additional Protocol I (from 1976) to the Geneva Convention of 1949 thus made it clear that mercenaries were not entitled to the status as combatants or POWs. It further defined who should count as mercenaries, namely

> [A]ny person who: (a) is specially recruited locally or abroad in order to fight in an armed conflict; (b) does, in fact, take a direct part in the hostilities; (c) is motivated to take part in the hostilities essentially by the desire for private gain and, in fact, is promised, by or on behalf of a Party to the conflict,

DOI: 10.1057/9781137502797.0008

material compensation substantially in excess of that promised or paid to combatants of similar ranks and functions in the armed forces of that Party; (d) is neither a national of a Party to the conflict nor a resident of territory controlled by a Party to the conflict; (e) is not a member of the armed forces of a Party to the conflict; and (f) has not been sent by a State which is not a Party to the conflict on official duty as a member of its armed forces.[29]

This may be one of the reasons that modern-day contractors are eager to distinguish themselves from old-fashioned mercenaries, for example, by emphasising that they only have legitimate customers, operate under rigid controls, are (usually) not engaged in direct combat, and so on. While this may actually be the case of many PMCs, there are surely also cases of 'rogue mercenaries' as well as of companies straddling the borderline between these and the more 'civilianised' PMCs, including companies such as Executive Outcomes and Sandline, both of which are now defunct,[30] and the notorious Blackwater, which after its scandalous behaviour in Iraq was in 2009 renamed 'Xe Services' and the following year (under new owners and management) became 'Academi' which seems an insult to Plato as the founder of the first university under the same name.[31]

Notwithstanding the appalling behaviour of some of these PMCs and the dubious track record of many others, it seems almost certain that PMCs are here to stay which means that the questions of the legal status of contractors and their personnel cries out for (both national and international) clarification and regulation.[32]

4.2   Training camps for guerrillas and terrorists

In the all too widespread instances of hostility between neighbouring states, a state's neighbours often have a vested interest in weakening it; and this interest is almost always reciprocated. One way of achieving this is to support whoever is fighting against the incumbent regime in this state, regardless of whether this struggle is purely political or takes the form of an armed struggle.

In some cases, neighbouring states (and occasionally others) therefore offer some form of assistance to the resistance, for example, by granting its members sanctuary on their territory, as was, for instance, the case of the so-called 'Front Line States' in southern Africa most of whom hosted members of the African National Congress (ANC) who had been

DOI: 10.1057/9781137502797.0008

exiled by the apartheid regime in South Africa.[33] As far as the leaders are concerned they are rarely encamped, but if it is a matter of large numbers of rank-and-file guerrilla soldiers, these usually are,[34] sometimes by integrating them with the substantial number of the refugees who are a very frequent biproduct of an armed struggle, and to which we shall return in the next chapter. As a means of maintaining discipline, the ANC also established its own detention camps in some of its countries of exile,[35] as well as training camps for its military wing, *UmKhonto we Sizwe*, that is, the 'Spear of the Nation.'[36]

Although the Soviet Union supported the struggle of both the ANC and their regional allies,[37] they were not alone in sponsoring such 'proxy wars.' The US did pretty much the same on several occasions, for example, with their support for the *Contras* fighting against the Sandinista government of Nicaragua. The Contras also had training camps in neighbouring states such as Honduras.[38] While there were probably good reasons for other parts of the Nicaraguan population than the allies of the former Somoza dictatorship to be dissatisfied by the Sandinistas,[39] part of the attraction of the Contras was surely also the support they received from the US. Training camps for such insurgents in a proxy war are thus functional equivalents of military barracks, only located on another state's national territory, which may then also serve as military outposts for the distant great- or superpower patron.

Whereas the 'traditional' training camps have been for guerrillas and mainly featured more regular military techniques, plus ideological training, training camps for designated 'terrorists' seem to have been mainly devoted to ideological indoctrination, but also training various terrorist tactics.[40] The distinctions between the two camps are blurred, to say the least. The US thus until quite late classified the ANC as terrorist which logically meant treating the aforementioned training camps as terrorist training facilities.[41] Several countries have at various times allowed the establishment of training camps for groups which others have regarded as terrorist organisations. Colonel Gadaffi's Libya was for a long time regarded (with considerable justification) as the main culprit in this respect,[42] but countries such as Lebanon also has a long history of allowing training camps for *Hezbollah* fighters,[43] and first Sudan and then the Afghanistan of the Taliban allowed the establishment of al Qaeda training camps on their territories.[44] Although this surely merits attention from possible targets of terrorism, and may even warrant military responses, the effectiveness of such responses as the bombing of Libya in 1986, and

DOI: 10.1057/9781137502797.0008

Afghanistan in 1998 and then again in 2001 as counter-terrorist strategies seems more questionable. Do terrorists and their organisation actually need bases and 'homes' or can they find sanctuary by 'blending in' with the ordinary population, also in the West? To what extent is 'training' really required for their planned activities? And could whatever training may be indispensable be acquired in cyberspace.[45]

4.3   Counter-insurgencies, camps and strategic hamlets

Both guerrillas and terrorists are insurgents, but at least as frequently as such insurgents have made use of camps, the powers that be have done so in their counter-insurgency (COIN in contemporary strategic jargon) campaigns.

The reason for this is the most prominent social feature of guerrilla war, that is, the special relationship between the (especially rural) population and the guerrillas. Based on the experience of the difficulties experienced by the Napoleonic armies in suppressing the Spanish insurgents (resistance or freedom fighters, as we would probably call them today) in the Peninsular War,[46] classical strategic thinkers such as Antoine de Jomini and Carl von Clausewitz labelled them 'people's wars.' Having personally fought in the Peninsular War, the former described the strength of guerrilla war:

> No army, however disciplined, can contend successfully against such a system applied to a great nation, unless it be strong enough to hold all the essential points of the country, cover its communications, and at the same time furnish an active force sufficient to beat the enemy wherever he may present himself.[47]

Clausewitz was equally impressed by the strength of the guerrillas,[48] but the greatest guerrilla strategist of all was surely Mao Zedong, who wrote about the topic *in extenso*.[49] He came up with the famous formula for the relationship between guerrillas and the local (peasant) population, that 'the former may be likened to the water, the latter to the fish that inhabit it.'[50] The lesson usually drawn from this dictum by the adversaries of the guerrillas – be they colonial powers such as the Germans in Southwest Africa, that is, the present Namibia,[51] foreign invaders such as the Japanese in China in the 1930s or 'imperialists' such as the US in South

DOI: 10.1057/9781137502797.0008

Vietnam – has therefore been that the 'fish' must somehow be separated from the 'water', that is, the peasant population. The establishment of camps would seem to recommend themselves as a suitable means to this end, that is, simultaneously defeating the guerrillas and defending the peasantry – but before proceeding to this, is seems appropriate to briefly review the more distant past with a view to determining the 'usual' relationship between town and country in times of war and other armed struggles.

From a certain perspective towns might be seen as a sort of camps scattered across the vast countryside. Throughout the Middle Ages such urban settlements were usually heavily fortified, for example, by means of castles, stone walls, moats, and so on, which made them suitable places of refuge during wars for the vast majority of the population who lived as peasants in the surrounding countryside.[52] The same was the case of the palisade-fenced craals (*kraals* in Dutch/Afrikaans) in southern Africa, which also provided some protection for peasants from the surrounded countryside during wars such as the colonial Zulu and Matabele wars as well as the Boer War mentioned in Chapter 3.[53]

Gradually, however, these fortified towns became obsolete, also as a result of the growth of the modern state which presupposed that the crown was able to bring insubordinate feudal rulers to heel, and the spread of heavy artillery capable of penetrating the defences of these castles. Rather than defending cities by military means, another form of defence then made its appearance, which arguably represented the exact opposite.

Building on customary humanitarian law pertaining to siege warfare, both the 1899 and the 1907 Hague Conventions thus contained provisions for declaring cities 'undefended' (previously called 'open'), which made them illegal targets of military attack by land forces as well as aerial bombardment. Not all cities were 'covered' by this legal protection (if so it was) as this required, as a minimum, that the city was declared 'undefended' with the implication that the respective enemy would be free to occupy it at will.[54] The 'absolute wars' of the twentieth century, in turn, made cities their main targets, with gruesome examples such as the Japanese 'Rape of Nanking'[55] and WWII events such as the siege of Leningrad, the fire-bombings of Hamburg and Tokyo, the bombing of Dresden and, last but not least, the nuclear bombings of Hiroshima and Nagasaki in August 1945 demonstrated the dangers flowing from concentration of the civilian population in cities.[56] Cities now appeared as traps and dispersal into the countryside now seemed to provide much better protection for civilians, even the urban population itself.

The need to separate insurgents from the civilian (mainly rural) population led to the invention of 'strategic hamlets.'[57] It seems to have all begun with the British counter-insurgency war in Malaya, during which the colonial power constructed resettlement areas, rebranded as 'new villages,' into which they forcefully moved a large proportion of the rural population.[58] The Americans emulated this strategy in Vietnam,[59] where they launched a policy of resettlement of peasants in 'strategic hamlets,' thus effectively dividing the South Vietnamese countryside into protected 'insides' and an 'outside' representing a free shooting range, where virtually everybody was treated as potential Viet Cong members and ipso facto as legitimate targets.[60] The French had done something similar in the course of their protracted counter-insurgency war in Algeria, where they established *villages de regroupement* on a grand scale to separate the FLN (*Front de Libération Nationale*, i.e. National Liberation Front) from its rural constituency,[61] a policy also emulated by various Third World dictatorships such as the one in Guatemala.[62]

Besides serving to separate the guerrilla from the rural population, fortified villages might, at least in principle, also be suitable means of 'social engineering' as they might contribute to 'capturing' what Göran Hydén (analysing the Tanzanian *Ujamaa* villagisation program) called 'the uncaptured peasantry.'[63] The basic problem, to which this was ostensibly a solution was one addressed by Karl Marx in his *Eighteenth Brumaire of Louis Bonaparte* in which he derogatively compared the small peasants of France to 'sacks of potatoes.'

> The small-holding peasants form an enormous mass whose members live in similar conditions but without entering into manifold relations with each other. Their mode of production isolates them from one another instead of bringing them into mutual intercourse. (...) Each individual peasant family is almost self-sufficient, directly produces most of its consumer needs, and thus acquires its means of life more through an exchange with nature than in intercourse with society. A small holding, the peasant and his family; beside it another small holding, another peasant and another family. (...) Thus the great mass of the French nation is formed by the simple addition of homologous magnitudes, much as potatoes in a sack form a sack of potatoes.[64]

Ever since, Marxist regimes have struggled with the problem of how to integrate these 'potatoes' in their reformed and collectivised societies, for example, via camp-like collective farms or communes. However

DOI: 10.1057/9781137502797.0008

persuasive their schemes (partly inspired by those of 'utopian socialists' such as Charles Fourier's *phalanstères*)[65] may have looked on paper, in practice the results and consequences of such schemes have ranged from great disappointments to unmitigated disasters. In the USSR the peasants evidently preferred to slaughter and eat their livestock rather than handing it over to collective farms, and their Chinese counter-parts clearly felt the same – in both cases with absolutely catastrophic consequences in the form of famines with death-tolls running into the millions.[66] They were only exceeded in brutality by the collectivisation movement of the *Khmer Rouge* in Cambodia, which not only forcefully drove the urban population into the countryside, but also forced the original rural population into communes.[67] These disastrous failures, however, did not dissuade the (partly Marxist) *Dergue* regime in Ethiopia from attempting the same, almost simultaneously with the Cambodian disaster and, similarly, with a 'Red Terror' campaign as a companion and severe famine as a result.[68]

While all of these attempts have proved catastrophic, at the disappointment end of the scale we find, besides the *Ujamaa* programme in Tanzania, the *Kibbutz* movement among the *Yishuv* in the British mandate territory of Palestine and subsequently taken over by the new state of Israel. These Kibbutzes were rural communes, partly resembling the *phalanstères* of the aforementioned Fourier and were thus means to the end of social reform, but they also served another purpose, that of colonisation, as they were often established on land previously owned by and therefore still contested by the indigenous Palestinian population. Moreover, the Jewish immigrants, and their inhabitants were, unlike most of those mentioned above, voluntary and often quite enthusiastic.[69] The fact that the *Kibbutzim* were both fenced and fortified made them ideal contributors to the national defence of Israel as well as for creating 'facts on the ground.'[70]

4.4 Summary

We have thus seen that both actual camps and camp-like institutions have played important, but very varied roles in connection with wars and other armed conflicts: Some camps are used to separate legitimate targets (i.e., combatants) from illegitimate ones, that is, civilians or, more precisely, non-combatants, as is done by relocating the latter into

DOI: 10.1057/9781137502797.0008

strategic hamlets; but there are also camps (*in casu* POW camps and Red Cross-administered hospitals and other 'humanitarian spaces')[71] for the intermediate category of former combatants, that is, soldiers who have surrendered or otherwise rendered *hors de combat*. Some of the fenced villages in the rural parts of countries at war or undergoing dramatic changes (typically following a revolution) have also been used for large-scale social engineering, for example, via compulsory collectivisation – almost always unsuccessful and quite often with catastrophic consequences.

Notes

1   M. Shaw (2003) *War and Genocide: Organized Killing in Modern Society* (Cambridge: Polity Press).

2   H.S. Levie (1993) 'Prisoner of War,' in T.N. Dupuy (ed.) *International Military and Defense Encyclopedia* (Washington, DC: Brassey's), 5, 2185–2190; I.D. de Lupis (1987) *The Law of War* (Cambridge: Cambridge University Press), 281–293; L.C. Green (1993) *The Contemporary Law of Armed Conflict* (Manchester: Manchester University Press), 188–206; H. McCoubrey and N.D. White (1992) *International Law and Armed Conflict* (Aldershot: Dartmouth), 268–273.

3   Created by the author, mainly based on the ICRC's database *Treaties and States Parties to Such Treaties* at www.icrc.org/ihl.

4   T. Gill (2013) 'Chivalry: A Principle of the Law of Armed Conflict,' in M. Matthee et al. (eds.) *Armed Conflict and International Law: In Search of a Human Face* (The Hague: Asser Press), 33–51; R.C. Stacey (1994) 'The Age of Chivalry,' in M. Howard et al. (eds.) *The Laws of War: Constraints on Warfare in the Western World* (New Haven, CT: Yale University Press), 27–39; G. Parker 'Early Modern Europe,' ibid., 40–58.

5   J.J. Turner (1981) *Just War Tradition and the Restraint of War: A Moral and Political Inquiry* (Princeton, NJ: Princeton University Press); idem (1987) *The Quest for Peace: Three Moral Traditions in Western Cultural History* (Princeton, NJ: Princeton University Press); idem (1999) *Morality and Contemporary Warfare* (New Haven, CT: Yale University Press); J.B. Elshtain, ed. (1992) *Just War Theory* (Oxford: Blackwell); T. Nardin, ed. (1996) *The Ethics of War and Peace: Religious and Secular Perspectives* (Princeton, NJ: Princeton University Press).

6   J. Finnis (1996) 'The Ethics of War and Peace in the Catholic Natural Law Tradition,' in Nardin, *Ethics of War and Peace* (n. 5), 15–39; J. Boyle (1996) 'Just War Thinking in Catholic Natural Law,' ibid., 40–53.

DOI: 10.1057/9781137502797.0008

7   D.R. Smock, ed. (1992) *Religious Perspectives on War: Christian, Muslim, and Jewish Attitudes toward Force after the Gulf War* (Washington, DC: USIP); idem, ed. (1993) *Perspectives on Pacifism: Christian, Jewish, and Muslim Views on Nonviolence and International Conflict* (Washington, DC: USIP); J.J. Turner (2003) 'Aquinas and Luther on War and Peace: Sovereign Authority and the Use of Armed Force,' *Journal of Religious Ethics*, 31:1, 3–20; T. George (1984) 'War and Peace in the Puritan Tradition,' *Church History*, 53:4, 492–503; M. Walzer (1996) 'War and Peace in the Jewish Tradition,' in Nardin, *Ethics of War and Peace* (n. 5), 95–114; A. Ravitzky (1996) 'Prohibited Wars in the Jewish Tradition,' ibid., 115–127; B. Tibi (1996) 'War and Peace in Islam,' ibid., 128–145; S.H. Hashmi (1996) 'Interpreting the Islamic Ethics of War and Peace,' ibid., 146–166.

8   R. Kolb (1997) 'Origin of the Twin Terms *jus ad bellum/jus in bello*,' *International Review of the Red Cross*, 37, special issue 320, 553–562; M. Sassòli (2007) '*Ius ad Bellum* and *Ius in Bello*: The Separation between the Legality of the Use of Force and Humanitarian Rules to Be Respected in Warfare: Crucial or Outdated?' in M. Schmitt and J. Pejic (eds.) *International Law and Armed Conflict: Exploring the Faultlines. Essays in Honour of Yoram Dinstein* (Leiden: Martinus Nijhoff Publishers), 241–264.

9   T. Meron (1987) 'The Geneva Conventions as Customary Law,' *American Journal of International Law*, 81:2, 348–370; idem (2005) 'Revival of Customary Humanitarian Law,' *American Journal of Customary Humanitarian Law*, 99:4, 817–834.

10 C. Moorehead (1998) *Dunant's Dream: War, Switzerland and the History of the Red Cross* (New York: Harper Collins); J.F. Hutchinson (1996) *Champions of Charity: War and the Rise of the Red Cross* (Boulder, CO: Westview); M. Barnett (2011) *Empire of Humanity: A History of Humanitarianism* (Ithaca, NY: Cornell University Press), 76–94.

11 D.P. Forsythe (1976) 'The Red Cross as a Transnational Movement: Conserving and Changing the Nation-State System,' *International Organization*, 30:4, 607–630.

12 J-J. Rousseau (1923) *The Social Contract and Discourses*, at http://lf-oll. s3.amazonaws.com/titles/638/ 0132_Bk.pdf (Book I, Chapter IV).

13 B. Rieffer-Flanagan (2009) 'Is Neutral Humanitarianism Dead? Red Cross Neutrality: Walking the Tightrope of Neutral Humanitarianism,' *Human Rights Quarterly*, 31:4, 888–915; Z. Daboné (2011) 'International Law: Armed Groups in a State-Centric System,' *International Review of the Red Cross*, 93:882, 395–424; J.K. Kleffner (2011) 'The Applicability of International Humanitarian Law to Organized Armed Groups,' ibid., 443–461; M.N. Schmitt (2007) 'Asymmetrical Warfare and International Humanitarian Law,' in W. Heintschel von Heinegg and V. Eppig (eds.) *International Humanitarian Law Facing New Challenges* (New York: Springer), 17–48.

DOI: 10.1057/9781137502797.0008

14 G. Daly (2004) 'Napoleon's Lost Legions: French Prisoners of War in Britain, 1803–1814,' *History*, 89:295, 361–380; H. Mytum and N. Hall (2013) 'Norman Cross: Designing and Operating an Eighteenth-Century British Prisoner of War Camp,' in H. Mytum and G. Carr, eds, *Prisoners of War* (New York: Springer), 75–93.

15 J.H. Jameson (2013) 'Artifacts of Internment: Archaeology and Interpretation at Two American Civil War Prisoner-of-War Sites,' in Mytum and Carr, *Prisoners of War* (n. 14), 23–40; P.G. Avery and P.L. Garrow (2013) 'Life and Death at the Florence Stockade, American Civil War, Prisoner of War Camp, South Carolina,' ibid., 41–58.

16 G.H. Davis (1993) 'National Red Cross Societies and Prisoners of War in Russia, 1914–18,' *Journal of Contemporary History*, 28:1, 31–52; S.P. MacKenzie (1994) 'The Treatment of Prisoners of War in World War II,' *Journal of Modern History*, 66:3, 487–520.

17 N. Ferguson (2004) 'Prisoner Taking and Prisoner Killing in the Age of Total War: Towards a Political Economy of Military Defeat,' *War in History*, 11:2, 148–192; B. Dollery and C.R. Parsons: 'Prisoner Taking and Prisoner Killing: A Comment on Ferguson's Political Economy Approach,' ibid., 14:4, 499–512.

18 K.C. Berkhoff (2001) 'The 'Russian' Prisoners of War in Nazi-Ruled Ukraine as Victims of Genocidal Massacre,' *Holocaust and Genocide Studies*, 15:1, 1–32; idem (2005) 'The Mass Murder of Soviet Prisoners of War and the Holocaust: How Were They Related?' *Kritika*, 6:4, 789–796.

19 K. Lowe (2013) *Savage Continent: Europe in the Aftermath of World War II* (London: Penguin), 111–124.

20 Ibid., 122.

21 An analysis written when millions remained in POW camps is R.A. Radford (1945) 'The Economic Organization of a P.O.W. Camp,' *Economica*, 12:48, 189–201.

22 G. Sanford (2005) *Katyn: The Whole Truth about the Soviet Massacre* (London: Routledge), 35–63, 90–123; K. Karski (2011) 'The Katyn Massacre as a Crime of Genocide in International Law,' *Polish Quarterly of International Affairs*, 4, 5–37.

23 J.P. Bialke (2004) 'Al-Qaeda and Taleban: Unlawful Combatant Detainees, Unlawful Belligerence, and the International Laws of Armed Conflict,' *Air Force Law Review*, 55:1, 1–86; S. Zachary (2005) 'Between the Geneva Conventions: Where Does the Unlawful Combatant Belong?' *Israel Law Review*, 38:1–2, 378–417; L.N. Sadat (2009) 'A Presumption of Guilt: The Unlawful Enemy Combatant and the U.S. War on Terror,' *Denver Journal of International Law and Policy*, 37:4, 539–554.

24 D.M. Amann (2004) 'Guantanamo,' *Columbia Journal of Transnational Law*, 42:2, 263–348; S.D. O'Connor (2008) 'Guantanamo Bay: Legal Black Hole,' *Canterbury Law Review*, 14:2, 207–216.

25 T. Yin (2011) "Anything but Bush': The Obama Administration and Guantanamo Bay,' *Harvard Journal of Law and Public Policy*, 34:2, 453–492.

DOI: 10.1057/9781137502797.0008

26   C.J. Mandernach (2007) 'Warriors without Law: Embracing a Spectrum
of Status for Military Actors,' *Appalachian Journal of Law*, 7:1, 137–178; S.
Gul (2006) 'The Secretary Will Deny All Knowledge of Your Actions: The
Use of Military Contractors and the Implications for State and Political
Accountability,' *Lewis and Clark Law Review*, 10:2, 287–312.

27   R. Mandel (2002) *Armies without States: The Privatization of Security* (Boulder,
CO: Lynne Rienner); P.W. Singer (2003) *Corporate Warriors: The Rise of
the Privatized Military Industry* (Ithaca, NY: Cornell University Press); K.
Silverstein (2000) *Private Warriors* (London: Verso).

28   A.H. De Wolf (2006) 'Modern Condottieri in Iraq: Privatizing War from
the Perspective of International and Human Rights Law,' *Indiana Journal of
Global Legal Studies*, 13:2, 315–356; D.P. Ridlon (2008) 'Contractors or Illegal
Combatants? The Status of Armed Contractors in Iraq,' *Air Force Law Review*,
62, 199–253.

29   Green, *Contemporary Law of Armed Conflict* (n. 2) 111–114.

30   H.M. Howe (1998) 'Private Security Forces and African Stability: the Case
of Executive Outcomes,' *Journal of Modern African Studies*, 36:2, 307–331; A-F.
Musah (2000) 'A Country under Siege: State Decay and Corporate Military
Intervention in Sierra Leone,' in idem and J.K. Fayemi (eds.) *Mercenaries: An
African Security Dilemma* (London: Pluto), 76–116.

31   J. Scahill (2007) *Blackwater: The Rise of the World's Most Powerful Mercenary
Army* (London: Serpent's Tail); P. Jenkins (2009) 'How to Clear Up
Blackwater: Bringing Effective Regulation to the Private Military Industry,'
Temple International and Comparative Law Journal, 23:1, 177–204; J.T.
Mlimarcik (2006) 'Private Military Contractors and Justice: A Look at the
Industry, Blackwater, and the Falluja Incident,' *Regent Journal of International
Law*, 4:1, 129–147.

32   J.M. Maogoto and B. Sheehy (2005) 'Contemporary Private Military Firms
under International Law: An Unregulated 'Gold Rush',' *Adelaide Law Review*,
26:2 , 245–269; idem and idem (2009) 'Private Military Companies and
International Law: Building New Ladders of Legal Accountability and
Responsibility,' *Cardoso Journal of Conflict Resolution*, 11:1, 99–132; B.O. Barrie
(2004) 'Private Military Firms and Mercenaries: Potential for Liability
under International Law,' *Tilburg Foreign Law Review*, 12:4, 324–347; C.
Kinsey (2005): 'Regulation and Control of Private Military Companies: The
Legislative Dimension,' *Contemporary Security Policy*, 26:1, 84–102; A. Faite
(2004) 'Involvement of Private Contractors in Armed Conflict: Implications
under International Humanitarian Law,' *Defence Studies*, 4:2, 166–183.

33   S. Ellis and T. Sechaba (1992) *Comrades against Apartheid: The ANC and the
South African Communist Party in Exile* (London: James Currey).

34   S. Ellis (1994) 'Mbokodo: Security in ANC Camps, 1961–1990,' *African Affairs*,
93:371, 279–298.

DOI: 10.1057/9781137502797.0008

35 T. Cleveland, (2005) "We Still Want the Truth": The ANC's Angolan Detention Camps and Post-Apartheid Memory,' *Comparative Studies of South Asia, Africa and the Middle East*, 25:1, 63–78; P. Trewhela (2010) *Inside Quatro: Uncovering the Exile History of the ANC and SWAPO* (Auckland Park: Jacana Media), 63–90.

36 T. Motumi (1994) 'Umkhonto we Sizwe: Structure, Training and Force Levels,' *African Defence Review*, 18, 1–11.

37 C. Stevens (1976) 'The Soviet Union and Angola,' *African Affairs*, 75:299, 137–151; V. Shubin and A. Tokarev (2001) 'War in Angola: A Soviet Dimension,' *Review of African Political Economy*, 28:90, 607–618.

38 K. Roberts (1990) 'Bullying and Bargaining: The United States, Nicaragua, and Conflict Resolution in Central America,' *International Security*, 15:2, 67–102; W.M. LeoGrande (1998) *Our Own Backyard: The United States in Central America, 1977–1992* (Chapel Hill, NC: University of North Carolina Press); S. Peterson and C. Wenk (2001) 'Domestic Institutional Change and Foreign Policy: A Comparative Study of U.S. Intervention in Guatemala and Nicaragua,' *Security Studies*, 11:1, 53–76; P. Kornbluh (1992) 'Nicaragua,' in P.J. Schraeder (ed.) *Intervention into the 1990s: U.S. Foreign Policy in the Third World*. 2nd ed. (Boulder, CO: Lynne Rienner), 285–301; H.H. Ransom (1992) 'Covert Intervention,' ibid., 113–129; P.J. Schraeder (1992) 'Paramilitary Intervention,' ibid., 131–151.

39 For a more favourable view see R.P. Hager, Jr. (1998) 'The Origins of the 'Contra War' in Nicaragua: The Results of a Failed Development Model,' *Terrorism and Political Violence*, 10:1, 133–164.

40 D. Byman (2007) *Deadly Connections: States that Sponsor Terrorism* (Cambridge: Cambridge University Press); D.B. Carter (2012) 'A Blessing or a Curse? State Support for Terrorist Groups,' *International Organization*, 66:1, 129–151; P. Nesser (2008) 'How Did Europe's Global Jihadis Obtain Training for Their Militant Causes,' *Terrorism and Political Violence*, 20:2, 234–256; B.A. Jackson et al. (2005) *Aptitude for Destruction*, 1–2 (Santa Monica, CA: Rand).

41 J. Denton (1986) 'The Role of the Senate Subcommittee on Security and Terrorism in the Development of U.S. Policy against Terrorism,' *Ohio Northern University Law Review*, 13:1, 19–26.

42 P. Jenkins (1988) 'Whose Terrorists? Libya and State Criminality,' *Contemporary Crises*, 12:1, 5–24; Y. Ronen (2002) 'Qadhafi and Militant Islamism: Unprecedented Conflict,' *Middle Eastern Studies*, 38:4, 1–16.

43 M. Ranstorp (2005) 'The Hisballah Training Camps in Lebanon,' in J.J.F. Forest (ed.) *The Making of a Terrorist, II: Recruitment, Training, and Root Causes* (Westport, CT: Praeger), 243–262.

44 A. Stenersen (2011) 'Al Qaeda's Foot Soldiers: A Study of the Biographies of Foreign Fighters Killed in Afghanistan and Pakistan Between 2002 and 2006,' *Studies in Conflict and Terrorism*, 34:3, 171–198; P. Bergen and P. Cruickshank (2012) 'Revisiting the Early Al Qaeda: An Updated Account of Its Formative

DOI: 10.1057/9781137502797.0008

Years,' ibid., 35:1, 1–36; B.G. Williams (2008) 'Talibanistan: History of a Transnational Terrorist Sanctuary,' *Civil Wars*, 10:1, 40–59; J. Burke (2004) *Al Qaeda: The True Story of Radical Islam* (Harmondsworth: Penguin), 94–6, 258–261; L. Wright (2006) *The Looming Tower: Al Qaeda and the Road to 9/11* (New York: Vintage), 128–130, 322–323, 340–342.

45   R. Takeyh and N. Gvosdev (2002) 'Do Terrorist Networks Need a Home?' *Washington Quarterly*, 25:2, 97–108; A. Stenersen (2008) 'The Internet: A Virtual Training Camp?' *Terrorism and Political Violence*, 20:2, 215–233.

46   D. Gates (1986) *The Spanish Ulcer: A History of the Peninsular War* (New York: W.W. Norton).

47   A-H. de Jomini (1978) 'Précis de l'art de guerre,' in W. Laqueur (ed.) *The Guerilla Reader: A Historical Anthology* (London: Wildwood House), 42–44.

48   C. von Clausewitz (1980) *Vom Kriege* (Frankfurt a.M.: Ullstein Verlag), 43, 193–198 (Book I.2 and III.16); W. Hahlweg (1986) 'Clausewitz and Guerilla Warfare,' *Journal of Strategic Studies*, 9:2–3, 127–133.

49   Mao Tse-Tung (1975) 'Problems of Strategy in China's Revolutionary War,' in *Selected Works of Mao Tse-Tung*, 1 (Peking: Foreign Languages Press), 179–254; idem 'Problems of Strategy in Guerrilla War against Japan,' ibid., 2, 79–112; idem 'On Protracted War,' ibid., 113–194; idem 'Problems of War and Strategy,' ibid., 219–235.

50   Idem (1937) 'On Guerilla Warfare,' at www.marxists.org/reference/archive/mao/works/1937/guerrilla-warfare/ch06.htm.

51   J.B. Gewald (1999) *Herero Heroes* (Oxford: James Currey), 185–191, 193–204, 246–260.

52   G.J. Ashworth (1991) *War and the City* (London: Routledge); J.H. Beeler (1956) 'Castles and Strategy in Norman and Early Angevin England,' *Speculum*, 31:4, 581–601; R.A. Brown (1955) 'Royal Castle-Building in England, 1154–1216,' *English Historical Review*, 70:27, 353–398; B.S. Bachrach (1994) 'Medieval Siege Warfare: A Reconnaissance,' *Journal of Military History*, 58:1, 119–133; J.A. Lynne (1995) 'The *Trace Italienne* and the Growth of Armies: The French Case,' in C. Rogers (ed.) *The Military Revolution Debate: Readings on the Military Transformation of Early Modern Europe* (Boulder, CO: Westview), 169–199.

53   R. Elphick (1977) *Kraal and Castle: Khoikhoi and the Founding of White South Africa* (New Haven, CT: Yale University Press); J. Laband (1995) *Rope of Sand: The Rise and Fall of the Zulu Kingdom in the Nineteenth Century* (Jeppestown: Jonathan Ball), 7–9; G.L. Dodds (1998) *The Zulus and Matabele: Warrior Nations* (London: Arms and Armour Press), 17–19; 155–157.

54   H.W. Elliott (1995) 'Open Cities and (Un)Defended Places,' *Army Lawyer*, 1994:4, 39–50; K.H. Kunzmann (1965) 'Militärisches Objekt und Unverteidigte Stadt,' *Military Law and Law of War Review*, 4:1, 103–132; M.C. Waxman (1999) 'Siegecraft and Surrender: The Law and Strategy of Cities as

DOI: 10.1057/9781137502797.0008

Targets', *Virginia Journal of International Law*, 39:2, 353–424; J.F. Elkin (1980) 'The Application of the Open City Concept to Rome 1942–1944', *Air Force Law Review*, 22:2, 188–200.

55 I. Chang (1997) *The Rape of Nanking: The Forgotten Holocaust of World War II* (Harmondsworth: Penguin).

56 R.A. Pape (1996) *Bombing to Win: Air Power and Coercion in War* (Ithaca, NY: Cornell University Press), 254–313; W.R. Murray (1996) 'Strategic Bombing: The British, American, and German Experiences', in idem and A.R. Millett (eds.) *Military Innovation in the Interwar Period* (Cambridge: Cambridge University Press), 144–190; G.Alperovitz (1985) *Atomic Diplomacy: Hiroshima and Potsdam. The Use of the Atomic Bomb and the American Confrontation with Soviet Power* (Harmondsworth: Penguin); J.S. Walker (1997) *Prompt and Utter Destruction: Truman and the Use of Atomic Bombs against Japan* (Chapel Hill, NC: University of North Carolina Press).

57 R. Marston (1979) 'Resettlement as a Counter-Revolutionary Technique', *RUSI Journal*, 124:4, 46–50.

58 P. Busch (2002) 'Killing the 'Vietcong': The British Advisory Mission and the Strategic Hamlet Programme', *Journal of Strategic Studies*, 25:1 135–162; K. Hack (2009) 'The Malayan Emergency as Counter-Insurgency Paradigm', ibid., 32:3, 383–414.

59 P. Sodhy (1987) 'The Malaysian Connection in the Vietnam War', *Contemporary Southeast Asia*, 9:1, 38–53; Y.F. Khong (1987) 'Seduction by Analogy in Vietnam: The Malaya and Korea Analogies', in K.W. Thompson (ed.) *Institutions and Leadership: Prospects for the Future* (Lanham, MD: University Press of America), 65–80.

60 M.E. Osborne (1965) *Strategic Hamlets in South Vietnam: A Survey and Comparison* (Ithaca, NY: Cornell University Southeast Asia Program); P.E. Catton (1999) 'Counter-Insurgency and Nation Building: The Strategic Hamlet Programme in South Vietnam, 1961–1963', *International History Review*, 21:4, 918–940; M. Maclear (1981) *Vietnam: The Ten Thousand Day War* (London: Thames-Methuen), 77–84; J.W. Gibson (1988) *The Perfect War: The War We Couldn't Lose and How We Did* (New York: Vintage), 69–89.

61 M. Bennoune (2001) 'La doctrine contre-révolutionnaire de la France et la paysannerie algérienne: Les champs de regroupement (1954–1962)', *Sud/Nord*, 1:14, 51–66; K. Sutton (1977) 'Population Resettlement: Traumatic Upheavals and the Algerian Experience', *Journal of Modern African Studies*, 15:2, 279–300; idem (1999) 'Army Administration Tensions over Algeria's Centres de Regroupement, 1954–1962', *British Journal of Middle Eastern Studies*, 26:2 (1999), 243–270; D. Galula (2006) *Pacification in Algeria, 1956–1958* (Santa Monica, CA: Rand); J. Frémaux (2012) 'The French Experience in Algeria: Doctrine, Violence and Lessons Learnt', *Civil Wars*, 14:1, 49–62; M. Alexander and J.F.V. Keiger (2002) 'France and the Algerian War: Strategy, Operations and

Diplomacy,' *Journal of Strategic Studies*, 25:2, 1–32; E.R. Wolf (1999) *Peasant Wars of the Twentieth Century* (Norman, OK: University of Oklahoma Press), 209–247.

62   F. Stepputat (1999) 'Politics of Displacement in Guatemala,' *Journal of Historical Sociology*, 12:1, 54–80.

63   G. Hydén (1980) *Beyond Ujamaa in Tanzania: Underdevelopment and an Uncaptured Peasantry* (London: Heinemann); T. Waters (1992) 'A Cultural Analysis of the Economy of Affection and the Uncaptured Peasantry in Tanzania,' *Journal of Modern African Studies*, 30:1, 163–175.

64   K. Marx (1852) 'The Eighteenth Brumaire of Louis Bonaparte,' at www. marxists.org/archive/marx/works/1852/18th-brumaire/ch07.htm; M. Duggett (1975) 'Marx on Peasants,' *Journal of Peasant Studies*, 2:2, 159–182; T. Shanin (1982) 'Defining Peasants: Conceptualisations and De-Conceptualisations: Old and New in a Marxist Debate,' *Sociological Review*, 30:3, 407–432.

65   C. Fourier (1969) *Textes Choisis* (Paris: éditions sociales), 135–158; M. Poster, ed. (1971) *Harmonian Man: Selected Writings of Charles Fourier* (New York: Anchor Books), 180–190.

66   On the USSR see R. Conquest (1986) *The Harvest of Sorrow: Soviet Collectivization and the Terror-Famine* (Oxford: Oxford University Press); L. Viola (1996) *Peasant Rebels under Stalin: Collectivization and the Culture of Peasant Resistance* (Oxford: Oxford University; M. Tauger (2004) 'Soviet Peasants and Collectivization, 1930–39: Resistance and Adaptation,' *Journal of Peasant Studies*, 31:3–4, 427–456. On China see F. Dikötter (2011) *Mao's Great Famine: The History of China's Most Devastating Catastrophe, 1958–62* (London: Bloomsbury); Wei Li (2005) 'The Great Leap Forward: Anatomy of a Central Planning Disaster,' *Journal of Political Economy*, 113:4, 840–877; D.T. Yang (2008) 'China's Agricultural Crisis and Famine of 1959–1961: A Survey and Comparison to Soviet Famines,' *Comparative Economic Studies*, 50:1, 1–29.

67   B. Kiernan (2008) *The Pol Pot Regime: Race, Power, and Genocide in Cambodia under the Khmer Rouge, 1975–79*. 3rd ed. (New Haven, CT: Yale University Press).

68   M. Stahl (1989) 'Capturing the Peasants through Cooperatives: The Case of Ethiopia,' *Review of African Political Economy*, 16:44, 27–46; M. Ottaway (1977) 'Land Reform in Ethiopia, 1974–1977,' *African Studies Review*, 20:3, 79–90; G. Tareke (2008) 'The Red Terror in Ethiopia: A Historical Aberration,' *Journal of Developing Societies*, 24:2, 183–206; P. Toggia (2012) 'The Revolutionary Endgame of Political Power: The Genealogy of 'Red Terror' in Ethiopia,' *African Identities*, 10:3, 265–280; M. Tegegn (2012) 'Mengistu's 'Red Terror',' ibid., 249–263.

69   Y. Amir (1969) 'The Effectiveness of the Kibbutz-Born Soldier in the Israel Defense Forces,' *Human Relations*, 22:4, 333–344; G. Forman (2006) 'Military Rule, Political Manipulation, and Jewish Settlement: Israeli Mechanisms

DOI: 10.1057/9781137502797.0008

for Controlling Nazareth in the 1950s,' *Journal of Israeli History*, 25:2, 335–359; S. Sandler (1993) *The State of Israel, the Land of Israel: The Statist and Ethnonational Dimensions of Foreign Policy* (Westport, CT: Greenwood Press).

70   Y. Ben-Artzi (2001) 'Kibbutz or Moshav? Priority Changes of Settlement Types in Israel, 1949–53,' *Israel Affairs*, 8:1–2, 163–176; E. Ben-Rafael (2011) 'Kibbutz: Survival at Risk,' *Israel Studies*, 17:2, 81–108; R. Russell et al. (2011) 'The Transformation of the Kibbutzim,' ibid., 16:2, 109–126; U. Zilbersheid (2007) 'The Israeli Kibbutz: From Utopia to Dystopia,' *Critique*, 35:3, 413–434; M-E. Spiro (2004) 'Utopia and Its Discontents: The Kibbutz and Its Historical Vicissitudes,' *American Anthropologist*, 106:3, 556–568.

71   M. Acuto (ed.) (2014) *Negotiating Relief: The Politics of Humanitarian Space* (London: Hurst).

DOI: 10.1057/9781137502797.0008

5
Camps for People in Flight

Abstract: *Camps play an important role in the international refugee regime alongside and as an alternative to asylum and repatriation. Established for the temporary custody and protection of refugees, protracted refugee situations camps come to function as permanent homes for refugees and internally displaced persons, that is, IDPs. Often refugee camps are militarised in the sense that fighters are recruited among the refugees by insurgents, which may even transform refugee camps into training camps and bases for rebel groups. In response, refugee and internally displaced person (IDP) camps are sometimes attacked as part of counter-insurgency campaigns. The chapter also deals with the phenomenon of 'boat people,' that is, refugees arriving by sea.*

Keywords: asylum; boat people; environmental refugees; humanitarianism; internally displaced persons; protracted refugee situations; refugee camps; Refugee Convention; refugee regime; refugees; refugee warriors; Sabra and Shatila; securitisation

Møller, Bjørn. *Refugees, Prisoners and Camps: A Functional Analysis of the Phenomenon of Encampment.* Basingstoke: Palgrave Macmillan, 2015. DOI: 10.1057/9781137502797.0009.

DOI: 10.1057/9781137502797.0009

Among the most widespread forms of camps in today's world are those established for humanitarian reasons as places of shelter for people in flight including, but not limited to, people legally qualifying as refugees. These camps are also among the best researched camps which have evidently attracted quite a number of not least anthropologists. They also form 'humanitarian spaces,' where well-intentioned benefactors provide relief to people, both needing and deserving all the help they can get. Unfortunately, there is more to it than that as we shall see.

5.1   The refugee regime

The phenomena of refugees, exile and asylum all have a very long history, as do the various social and religious norms and customs pertaining to their treatment.[1] Not only has religion for centuries been a reason for people to flee persecution, as was the case of the French Huguenots in the seventeenth century,[2] but religion may also oblige people and states to offer hospitality to people in flight,[3] typically in the form of official or de facto asylum, that is, sanctuary. Christianity thus makes the caring for people forced to flee their homes a moral and religious obligation.[4] Pope Pius XII thus reminded the world's Catholics that

> The émigré Holy Family of Nazareth, fleeing into Egypt, is the archetype of every refugee family. Jesus, Mary and Joseph, living in exile in Egypt to escape the fury of an evil king, are, for all times and all places, the models and protectors of every migrant, alien and refugee of whatever kind who, whether compelled by fear of persecution or by want, is forced to leave his native land, his beloved parents and relatives, his close friends, and to seek a foreign soil.[5]

As far as the Islam is concerned, the Prophet himself was a refugee, seeking shelter from religious persecution in Medina in AD 622. Hence, Islam with its doctrine pertaining to *hijrah,* similarly, sees the provision of asylum as a divine obligation.[6]

The cornerstones of the contemporary international refugee regime were laid under the auspices of the League of Nations with the first international refugee convention adopted in 1933,[7] partly thanks to the work of the first High Commissioner for Refugees, the former Norwegian polar explorer Fridtjof Nansen.[8] Besides repatriation, for example, of refugees from the Russian civil war,[9] one of the main objectives was to find guidelines for the proper treatment of people fleeing totalitarian

DOI: 10.1057/9781137502797.0009

regimes such as the Stalinist Soviet Union and Nazi Germany along-side other dictatorships as well as dealing with the legacies of the 1915 Armenian genocide in Turkey.[10] Each European state was quite happy to leave most of this to the respective others,[11] both because of the economic costs involved and because of the expressive element which is implicit in the granting of asylum (*vide infra*).

Following a brief interlude after the World War II (WWII), during which the main organisation in charge of refugees was the United Nations' International Refugees Organization (IRO) of 1946,[12] a successor to the League's office of the High Commissioner was instituted in 1950, the office of the UNHCR (United Nations' High Commissioner for Refugees) which has remained the central organisation in the field.[13] In 1951 a new refugee convention (Convention Relating to the Status of Refugees) was adopted, to which most of the world's states have by now acceded, and to which in 1967 a protocol was appended which removed the temporal and geographical limitations found in the original convention, thereby removing its anachronistic features and ensuring its universal applica-bility.[14] These two represent the cornerstones of the contemporary inter-national refugee regime,[15] but besides the UNHCR another organisation, predating it by a couple of years, is also worth mentioning, that is, the special organisation established by the UN in 1949 to take charge of the Palestinian refugee problem, UNRWA (United Nations Relief and Works Agency for the Palestine Refugees in the Middle East).[16]

Moreover, a couple of regional refugee conventions have been adopted, complementing the 1951 convention in the sense of including additional categories of persons entitled to refugee status besides those already covered. The OAU (Organisation for African Unity) thus in a 'Convention Governing the Specific Aspects of Refugee Problems in Africa', adopted in 1969, expanded the definition of a refugee to 'Any person compelled to leave his/her country owing to external aggression, occupation, foreign domination or events seriously disturbing public order in either part or the whole of his country of origin or nationality,' thus both removing the criterion of *personal* persecution and those of the *reasons for* this persecution.[17] In the same vein a number of Latin American countries in 1984 adopted the 'Cartagena Declaration' which conferred eligibility for refugee status to 'Persons who flee their countries because their lives, safety or freedom have been threatened by generalised violence, foreign aggression, internal conflicts, massive violation of human rights or other circumstances which have seriously disturbed public order.'[18]

DOI: 10.1057/9781137502797.0009

The main element of the Refugee Convention is the norm of *non-refoulement* which prohibits returning an asylum applicant eligible for asylum or other protection to his country of origin, which in practice translates into a right to residence, either indefinitely or for a limited period – unless asylum applicants constitute a threat to the host state, for example, by being suspected of terrorist intentions. According to most analyses, there is even an exception to this exception, namely if the suspects risk being tortured or subjected to similar degrading treatment.[19]

Besides these conventions and organisations dealing explicitly and exclusively with refugees, a number of others arguably also belong to the refugee regime. This is, for instance, the 1959 'Convention Relating to the Status of Stateless Persons' and the 1961 'Convention on the Reduction of Statelessness,' both of which were intended to regulate the treatment of people who had either never been citizen of any state or, for whatever reason, been deprived of this citizenship, and who should either be entitled to citizenship in the country where they were born or be granted this status in their country of residence.[20] Furthermore, there are numerous other human rights conventions or treaties which may (by default) grant refugees some protection. Some pertain to special categories of humans such as children, the elderly, people with disabilities, women, members of indigenous and tribal peoples, people belonging to special (usually minority) races, ethnic groups or religious communities. Others pertain to all humans in special situations, a category to which refugees obviously belong as do detained or imprisoned people.[21]

There are also more general human rights legal instruments offering some legal protection to whoever is in flight, but do not qualify as refugees in the sense of the 1951 convention. This is especially the case of the European Convention on Human Rights (ECHR), adopted by the Council of Europe and the related judicial institution, the European Court of Human Rights (ECtHR), established in 1959, which has in several cases served as an international court of appeal in cases of a denial of asylum by a member state.[22] In 2011, for instance, the ECtHR found that 'the indiscriminate violence in Mogadishu in Somalia was of a sufficient level and intensity to pose a real risk to the life or person of any civilian there,' and that the UK was therefore obliged by the *non-refoulement* norm to grant the two plaintiffs (Sufi and Elmi) asylum or at least protection status.[23] As such ECtHR rulings often establish precedence; this one may bring Europe more in line with the OAU convention by

DOI: 10.1057/9781137502797.0009

relaxing the requirement of personal persecution, even though it was at the time of writing too early to tell.

The final, but in reality decisive, components of the regime are found at the state level, that is, in national legislation and practice. Surely, most states who have duly signed and ratified a binding convention have at least initially intended to abide by it, and either passed laws to implement the new norms or made the convention as such directly binding within their sovereign domain. However, the political mood often changes over time, as a result of which states may come to find the obligations incurred too cumbersome to fulfil or come to resent the limits they place around their sovereignty. They may then decide to reinterpret their obligations or even to blatantly disregard them, either by passing national legislation which is incompatible with the convention or by informally instituting practices which contravene them. This seems to be the case of certain European countries under duress such as Italy, Greece or Malta (and, to a lesser degree, perhaps also Spain) which receive, by far, most of the refugees coming from Africa and the Middle East to Europe. Rather than treating asylum-seekers decently, they seem to deliberately make life miserable for them in order to dissuade or deter others from following in their footsteps.[24]

This leaves the proverbial international community, or even regional organisations such as the European Union (EU), despite its quite extensive supranational powers, with only few options. The so-called 'Dublin Procedure' (laid down in three conventions usually called Dublin I, II and III from 1997, 2003 and 2013, respectively) allows member states to return asylum-seekers from beyond the EU to the country of their first entry, thus allowing for 'burden-shedding' and 'free-riding' on the part of the northern members of the community rather than the burden-sharing one might perhaps have expected, or desired for ethical reasons.[25]

Perhaps unfortunately, but due to various political considerations, the 1951 Convention's definition of refugees was quite restrictive,[26] as could be said about the Genocide Convention adopted two years earlier. The two share several features, but there are also significant differences – and they certainly share a central causal link, as at the time of their adoption a very large part of the refugees had fled the Holocaust and other genocidal atrocities which the Genocide Convention was adopted to prevent. While the Genocide Convention defined a genocide as attempts at destroying groups *as such*, for instance but not necessarily by killing their members, the Refugee Convention also referred to groups by defining

DOI: 10.1057/9781137502797.0009

a refugee as a person with 'well-founded fears of personal persecution' because of his or her belonging to a group. While most of the groups mentioned in the two conventions were the same, there were two 'omissions' in the Genocide Convention, that is, politically defined groups and the vague 'particular social group'. For a comparison see Table 5.1.

Since then, the main controversy seems to have been whether gender and/or sexual orientation should constitute such a group. While it is increasingly acknowledged that homo- and transsexuals (often referred to as 'LGBT' as the acronym for lesbians, gays, bisexuals, and transgender persons) are entitled to the label, not least because of the obvious persecution of these minorities in many countries,[27] it is more controversial to accept women as a 'particular social group,' if only because they make up approximately half of mankind and thus are no minority – but some nevertheless feel quite strongly that they should be.[28]

Just as the Genocide Convention does not, according to most experts, apply to what is usually referred to as a genocide, for example, the mass killings perpetrated by the Khmer Rouge in Cambodia in the 1970s (as the bulk of the victims were either killed for political reasons or at random, rather than as a result of a grand exterminatory plan),[29] the 1951 Refugee Convention does not automatically apply to all situations of mass flight such as the civil war in Syria, which had by the time of writing (September 2014) forcefully displaced approximately 6.5 million

TABLE 5.1   *The Refugee and Genocide Conventions*

Refugee Convention (1951), Art. 1:	Genocide Convention (1948), Art. 2o:
[T]he term refugee shall apply to any person who (...) owing to a well-founded fear of being persecuted for reasons of *race, religion, nationality, membership of a particular social group or political opinion,* is outside the country of his nationality and is unable or, owing to such fear, is unwilling to avail himself of the protection of that country; or who, not having a nationality and being outside the country of his former habitual residence as a result of such events, is unable or, owing to such fear, is unwilling to return to it.	Genocide means any of the following acts committed with intent to destroy, in whole or in part, *a national, ethnical, racial or religious group, as such*: (a) Killing members of the group; (b) Causing serious bodily or mental harm to members of the group; (c) Deliberately inflicting on the group conditions of life calculated to bring about its physical destruction in whole or in part; (d) Imposing measures intended to prevent births within the group; (e) Forcibly transferring children of the group to another group.

Source: ICRC's database *Treaties and States Parties to Such Treaties* at www.icrc.org/ihl

DOI: 10.1057/9781137502797.0009

people altogether, of which approximately 2.9 million had sought refuge in neighbouring countries, especially Lebanon (nearly 1.2 million), Jordan (more than 600,000), Turkey (more than 800,000), Iraq (more than 200,000) and Egypt (more than 130,000).[30]

Although camps have always played quite a prominent role in refugee protection (*vide infra*), there are other salient issues in this field, such as the institution of asylum (with the granting or refusal of which the present author is engaged on a part-time basis as member of the Danish Refugee Appeals Board), but which we shall largely bypass in the following. Granting asylum to an applicant is tantamount to pointing an accusatory finger at his or her home country,[31] which was actually appreciated during the cold war, when everybody fleeing the Eastern Block were hailed as freedom fighters, whose very flight constituted incriminating evidence against Communism.[32] It also helped that there were not all that many who fled – or rather escaped, as leaving one's country was viewed by the Communist regimes as treason. There had been much less enthusiasm about helping the millions of forcefully displaced persons in the wake of WWII, not least Germans fleeing in front of the advancing allied armies and then those who were expelled by the new regimes installed at war's end within the revised borders decided at Yalta and Potsdam.[33]

There are several limitations in this comprehensive refugee regime, besides what it shares with many other regimes, that is, the complete lack of, or the weaknesses of, enforcement mechanisms.[34] One of the assumptions of the refugee regime has always been that refugee status would be temporary, just as this was the assumption of Bertolt Brecht during his sojourn in the provincial Danish town of Svendborg as a fugitive from the Nazi regime in his native Germany:

> Don't drive any nail into the wall
> Just throw your coat on the chair
> Why buy food for four days?
> You will return tomorrow.[35]

As long as the refugees were expected to be either repatriated to their country of origin or naturalised in their country of residence, keeping them in camps (unlike Brecht and other intellectuals) for a while might seem to make sense. However, quite a few more recent refugee situations have proven very protracted,[36] which has made the camp option problematic as we shall see below.[37]

DOI: 10.1057/9781137502797.0009

5.2   Forgotten fugitives: IDPs, development and environmental refugees

From a humanitarian perspective one of the main shortcomings of the refugee regime described in the last section is that fairly large categories of people in flight are not covered by the quite narrow definition of 'refugees.'

First of all we have the category of people who are fleeing their homeland, only not driven by well-founded fears of persecution for the reasons listed in the Refugee Convention. Depending on where they seek refuge, they may be covered by more permissive regional conventions, or their country of refuge may interpret the *non-refoulement* principle so liberally that it does not deport people in grave danger, for example, of torture or of being killed as collateral victims of a war (*vide supra*).

Then we have the very large group of internally displaced persons (IDPs), comprising people fleeing for all sorts of reasons who have not (yet) crossed an international border. They were almost completely disregarded until the mid-1990s when people such as Francis Deng and Roberta Cohen placed the spotlight on them.[38] They pointed out that the IDPs might well be in even graver danger than 'real refugees,' if only because they are still residing in the country whose government is often responsible for their persecution. Moreover, these governments are not merely in a position to deny IDPs their protection and refuse to help meeting even their most basic needs for food, shelter and medical care, but they can also deny access for humanitarian agencies from abroad simply by playing the 'sovereignty card.' Hence the counter-discourse from international humanitarians such as Deng on, first, 'sovereignty as responsibility'[39] and then on the 'responsibility to protect' (often known as 'R2P') which was in 2005 endorsed by the UN in the non-binding, but nevertheless politically quite authoritative Summit Declaration. Even though this document does not explicitly say so, it is often interpreted as granting a conditional right, and perhaps even an obligation, for other states (or at least the UN itself) to intervene into the internal affairs of the country in question to help those not protected by their own state, including IDPs.[40]

The UNHCR has gradually moved into the IDP field even though it has no formal mandate to do this,[41] and it has published a set of (non-binding) *Guiding Principles on Internally Displacement*, in which IDPs are defined as

DOI: 10.1057/9781137502797.0009

Persons or groups of persons who have been forced or obliged to flee or to leave their homes or places of habitual residence, in particular as a result of or in order to avoid the effects of armed conflict, situations of generalised violence, violations of human rights or natural or human-made disasters, and who have not crossed an internationally recognised State border.[42]

Besides recommending to extend the same rights to IDPs as now enjoyed by refugees, it goes further than that by omitting the criteria of personal persecution and the reasons for this persecution, and by even including victims of natural disasters, to which we shall return shortly. Even further goes the 'Kampala Convention', adopted under the auspices of a special summit of the African Union (AU) in 2009 which entered into force in 2012.[43] Referring back to the above UNHCR guidelines and their definition of IDPs, it specifies the obligations of states to protect their citizens and obliges states to adopt legislation to implement them. It further obliges states to establish national early warning systems 'in the context of [a] continental early warning system,' and it holds out the threat of forceful intervention already contained in article 4h in the Constitutive Act of the African Union from 2002 – the world's first and furthest-reaching international legal instrument for R2P missions.[44]

While both the UNHCR Guidelines and the Kampala Convention do offer some legal protection for people forcefully displaced by 'violations of human rights' and 'natural or human-made disasters,' these broad terms raise the question where to draw the line, just as they may entail temptations to seek to broaden the criteria for refugee status for those fugitives who have crossed an international border: Do even minor violations by a state of the 1966 'International Covenant on Civil and Political Rights' entitle all its citizens to treatment as IDPs or even refugees, considering that some of these violations (e.g., 'unlawful interference with correspondence', listed in art. 17) rarely entail serious threats to their lives or well-being? And does, for instance, the 'right to work,' which is included as art. 6 in the very broad catalogue of socio-political rights of the 1966 'Covenant on Economic, Social and Cultural Rights' translate into an entitlement of all unemployed persons to IDP or refugee status? If so, should all illegal, undocumented or '*sans papiers*' cross-border migrants be treated as refugees?[45] It is far from obvious that these questions should be answered in the affirmative, and extremely unlikely that most states would think so.

As far as 'human-made disasters' are concerned, seen from a victim's perspective these may also include what looks more like (and may,

DOI: 10.1057/9781137502797.0009

indeed, be intended as) long-term improvements for society at large, as is the case of so-called 'development-induced displacement.' People may, for instance, be displaced from their homes or even their areas of residence by major construction programmes or other development-related environmental modifications.[46] Occasionally, people are even displaced for the sake of the environment, even for conservation, as may, for instance, happen when national parks are established for the sake of endangered species or to preserve endangered biospheres and habitats.[47]

The distinctions between man-made and 'natural disasters' are not always clear-cut, as is, for instance, the case of climate change, but from the vantage point of the victims this does not really matter. Some natural disasters such as earthquakes or tsunamis are surely not anthropogenic, even though some states may prepare their societies better than others for dealing with such calamities. It also includes people fleeing from natural disasters as well as slow-onset environmental problems such as droughts, and these non-conflict-related displacements primarily take place within countries, even though they might also make people cross borders in search of decent living conditions. Some of them are of rather short duration. People fleeing from disasters such as floods or earthquakes tend to return as fast as possible, whereas those displaced for the sake of development tend to be permanently relocated within their home country.

Even though these categories are sometimes referred to as 'environmental refugees' (or even 'climate change refugees'),[48] they would not qualify as refugees, even if they were to cross an international border. A possible exception to this rule might be the inhabitants of states which disappear completely, for example, small island states such as Tuvalu or Kiribati being flooded by rising sea levels,[49] thereby rendering their former citizens stateless, and ipso facto covered by the aforementioned conventions on statelessness. According to most analyses, however, such cases of 'modern Atlantises' are very unlikely,[50] but then again: the unfortunate inhabitants of the mythical Atlantis probably also regarded it as unlikely that 'the island of Atlantis (...) disappeared in the depth of the sea,' as happened according to Plato.[51]

5.3 Zooming out: the big picture of forced displacement

As appears from Table 5.2, the total refugee and IDP picture is dominated by a rather small number of countries with massive problems, very often

TABLE 5.2   *Refugee and IDP populations > 100,000 by country of origin (2012)*

Origin	Refugees	IDPs	Total
Afghanistan	2,585,605	486,298	3,071,903
Azerbaijan	15,914	600,336	616,250
Bosnia	51,939	103,449	155,388
Burundi	73,645	78,948	152,593
CAR	164,568	51,679	216,247
Chad	39,695	90,000	129,695
China	193,337	–	193,337
Colombia	394,122	3,943,509	4,337,631
Côte d'Iv.	100,689	45,000	145,689
DR Congo	509,396	2,669,069	3,178,465
Eritrea	285,142	–	285,142
Georgia	9,290	279,778	289,068
Iraq	746,440	1,131,810	1,878,250
Kenya	8,948	412,000	420,948
Kyrgyzstan	3,489	168,600	172,089
Mali	149,943	227,930	377,873
Myanmar	415,343	430,400	845,743
Pakistan	49,736	757,996	807,732
Russia	110,701	–	110,701
Serbia	158,164	227,821	385,985
Somalia	1,136,143	1,132,963	2,269,106
South Sud.	87,009	345,670	432,679
Sri Lanka	132,792	93,482	226,274
Sudan	569,212	1,873,300	2,442,512
Syria	728,542	2,016,500	2,745,042
Turkey	135,450	–	135,450
Viet Nam	336,945	–	336,945
W Sahara	116,452	–	116,452
Yemen	2,590	385,320	387,910
World	**10,500,241**	**17,670,368**	**28,170,609**

Source: Based on data from Table 2 in UNHCR, *Global Trends 2012: Statistics*, at www.unhcr.org/globaltrends/ 2012GlobalTrends_0913.zip.

in terms of both refugees and IDPs – simply because people often flee 'in steps,' first to somewhere else within their home country and then abroad.

As set out in Table 5.3, the vast majority of those who flee abroad, crossing a border, end up in immediately adjacent countries for the obvious reason that they can neither afford air tickets nor the 'services' offered by human traffickers which might take them to more distant and perhaps more attractive destinations such as Europe or North America. In the words of a respondent, 'I went as far as my money would take me.'[52] With no or very little money, refugees have to walk which means

TABLE 5.3   *Distribution of large refugee batches (ult. 2012)*

Origin	Neighbours		OECD	Others	Total	Neighbours
Afghanistan	Iran	824,087				
	Pakistan	1,637,740				
	Subtotal	2,461,827	84,131	9,633	2,555,591	96%
CAR	Cameroon	92,094				
	Chad	65,874				
	Subtotal	157,968				
China	India	100,003	77,370		177,373	56%
Colombia	Ecuador	122,964				
	Panama	15,723				
	Venezuela	203,563				
	Subtotal	342,250	35,329	10,305	387,884	88%
DRC	Angola	20,740				
	Burundi	41,349				
	CAR	10,662				
	Congo	89,424				
	Rwanda	57,857				
	South Sudan	18,296				
	Uganda	127,021				
	Tanzania	63,330				
	Zambia	14,871				
	Subtotal	443,550	17,791	19,630	480,971	92%
Eritrea	Ethiopia	63,771				
	Sudan	112,283				
	Subtotal	176,054	45,770	37,347	259,171	68%
Iraq	Iran	44,085				
	Jordan	63,037				
	Syria	471,418				
	Turkey	9,478				
	Subtotal	588,018	104,304	12,219	704,541	83%
Myanmar	Bangladesh	230,674				
	Thailand	83,317	–			
	Subtotal	313,991	–	92,342	406,333	77%
Serbia	Montenegro	8,504	125,315	–	133,819	6%
Somalia	Djibouti	18,289				
	Ethiopia	223,031				
	Kenya	512,069				
	Yemen	226,909				
	Subtotal	988,802	68,417	48,155	1,105,374	89%
Sri Lanka	India	67,165	48,602	48,602	164,369	41%
Sudan	Chad	306,960				
	Egypt	12,124				
	Ethiopia	27,175				
	South Sudan	176,834				
	Uganda	7,910				
	Subtotal	531,003	–	10,743	541,746	98%

Continued

DOI: 10.1057/9781137502797.0009

TABLE 5.3   *Continued*

Origin	Neighbours		OECD	Others	Total	Neighbours
Syria	Iraq	63,586				
	Jordan	238,798				
	Lebanon	126,939				
	Turkey	248,466				
	Subtotal	677,789	24,216	12,836	714,841	95%
Turkey	Iraq	15,496	101,660	–	117,156	13%
Viet Nam	China	300,897	32,404	–	333,301	90%
Western	Algeria	90,000	–	–		
Sahara	Mauritania	26,000	–	–		
	Subtotal	116,000	–	–	116,000	100%

Note: There are a few minor overlaps where OECD countries (e.g., Turkey) happen to also be neighbours, in which cases they have been counted as neighbours. Yemen is counted as a neighbour of Somalia, even though they do not share a land border. Palestinian refugees have been omitted, as most of them do not fall under UNHCR's mandate, but are handled by UNRWA.

Legend: CAR: Central African Republic; DRC: Democratic Republic of Congo; OECD: Members of the Organization for Economic Cooperation and Development, that is, Australia, Austria, Belgium, Canada, Chile, Czech Republic, Denmark, Estonia, Finland, France, Germany, Greece, Hungary, Iceland, Ireland, Israel, Italy, Japan, Luxembourg, Mexico, Netherlands, NZ, Norway, Poland, Portugal, Slovakia, Slovenia, South Korea, Spain, Sweden, Switzerland, Turkey, UK and the USA.

Source: Based on data from UNHCR, *Global Trends 2012* (n. 312), Table 5.

that they invariably end up just across the border. Moreover, the minuscule share of the refugees who reach the prosperous countries in the North usually represent the best resourced part of the total number of forcefully displaced people.

The number of IDPs dwarfs that of refugees. According to the Internal Displacement Monitoring Centre (IDMC) more than 32 million people were in 2012 displaced by natural disasters (See Table 5.4).

The IDMC's estimate of conflict-induced internal displacement in 2012 was 28.8 million, thus bringing the grand total of IDPs up to a record high of sixty million. The most heavily affected region was Africa with a total of 10.4 million followed by the Middle East and North Africa with 6 million (of which 2.4 million were from Syria) and South America with 5.8 million (of which Columbia stood for 4.9–5.5 million).[53]

To these figures should be added those of the world's oldest refugee population, that of the stateless Palestinians who have fled or been evicted from their homes in several rounds of the never-ending

TABLE 5.4   *Disaster-induced IDPs (2012)*

			'Top Ten'	
Africa		8,158,413		
Western	6,698,617		India	9,110,000
Eastern	794,278		Nigeria	6,111,580
Middle	578,537		China	5,730,800
Northern	84,581		Philippines	3,858,596
Southern	2,400		Pakistan	1,856,570
Americas		1,776,771	United States	900,932
Northern	900,932		Bangladesh	650,788
Caribbean	483,013		Niger	540,000
South	314,247		Chad	500,000
Central	78,579		Cuba	351,730
Asia		22,228,963	Others	2,755,625
Southern	11,826,569		**World**	**32,366,621**
Eastern	6,276,800			
South-Eastern	4,076,667			
Central	47,727			
Western	1,200			
Europe		73,925		
Southern	39,650			
Eastern	33,975			
Northern	300			
Oceania		128,549		
Melanesia	103,809			
Austr-NZ	16,450			
Polynesia	8,139			
Micronesia	151			
World		32,366,621		

Source: Based on data from Tables A3.1 and A3.2 on pp. 45–46 in Internal
Displacement Monitoring Centre (2013) *Global Estimates 2012:
People Displaced by Disasters* (Geneva: IDMC).

conflict between Israel and its Arab and Palestinian enemies. First
came what the Palestinians call *al-Nakba* ('the Catastrophe') in 1948,
that is, the founding of the Jewish state of Israel on the territory of
the British mandate territory of Palestine and the Arab-Israeli war that
followed. Then came the 1967 war, which brought further territories
with Palestinian populations under Israeli control, and ever since
there have been (in comparison) minor rounds of flight and eviction,
for example, in connection with Israeli attacks against Lebanon and
the two *Intifadas*, (uprisings) to which should be added the Jordanian

DOI: 10.1057/9781137502797.0009

onslaught on the Palestinians in September 1970.[54] The care of the Palestinian refugee population is the task of UNRWA (*vide supra*), established in 1949.[55] As of 1 January 2013, UNRWA was responsible for more than five million Palestinians of which approximately a third were residing in camps in Jordan, Lebanon, Syria, the West Bank and the Gaza Strip[56] as summarised in Table 5.5.

TABLE 5.5   *UNRWA-operated camps*

Gaza		West Bank			
Name	Residents	Name	Residents	Name	Residents
Beach	87,000	Aida	4,700	Ein el-Sultan	1,900
Bureij	34,000	Am'ari	10,500	Far'a	7,600
Deir el-Balah	21,000	Aqbat Jabr	6,400	Fawwar	8,000
Jabalia	110,000	Arroub	10,400	Jalazzone	11,000
Khan Younis	72,000	Askar	15,900	Jenin	16,000
Maghazi	24,000	Balata	23,600	Kalandia	11,000
Nuseirat	66,000	Beit Jibrin	1,000	Nur Shams	9,000
Rafah	104,000	Camp no. 1	6,750	Shu'fat	11,000
		Deir 'Ammar	2,400	Tulkarn	18,000
		Dheisheh	13,000		
Total	**51,800**			**Total**	**188,150**

Jordan		Lebanon		Syria	
Name	Residents	Name	Residents	Name	Residents
Amman New Camp	51,500	Beddawi	16,500	Dera'a	27,000
Baqa'a	104,000	Burj Barajneh	17,945	Ein el Tal	6,000
Husn	22,000	Burj Shemali	22,789	Hama	8,000
Irbid	25,000	Dbayeh	4,351	Homs	22,000
Jabal el-Hussein	29,000	Ein El Hilweh	54,116	Jarama	18,658
Jerash	24,000	El Buss	11,254	Khan Dunoun	10,000
Marka	53,000	Mar Elias	662	Khan Eshieh	20,000
Souf	20,000	Mieh Mieh	5,250	Latakia	10,000
Talbieh	7,000	Nahr el-Bared	5,558	Neirab	20,500
Zarqa	20,000	Rashidieh	31,478	Qabr Essit	23,700
		Shatila	9,842	Sbeineh	22,600
		Wavel	8,806	Yarmouk	148,500
Total	**355,500**		**188,551**		**336,958**

Source: Based on the data from UNRWA: 'Where We Work', at www.unrwa.org/where-we-work/

DOI: 10.1057/9781137502797.0009

5.4   Zooming in: life in and outside refugee and IDP camps

Refugee camps have always attracted considerable attention among anthropologists,[57] and they are, indeed, very important pieces in the global refugee or forced displacement puzzle, even though one might have wanted a greater attention to IDPs. The fact that IDP camps have only rarely been studied in the same manner may be due to the obvious problems involved in gaining access, as their camps are by definition within countries the government of which may either have deliberately displaced them or been unable to offer them protection. It is therefore understandably not exactly enthusiastical about critical scrutiny.

The encamped refugees are in many respects quite different from the camp inmates we have described in the previous chapters, as they are neither incarcerated for anything that they have done nor even for what they are, nor locked up with a view to being exterminated, nor even placed in camps as prisoners-of-war (POWs) for the remainder of a war still being fought or in preparation of a future one. They are civilians pure and simple who are being assisted and catered for by humanitarians with sincere intentions to help them, at the very least in the sense of keeping them alive.

As the refugee phenomenon is thus one of 'innocent people' in dire straits being helped by 'good people,' one might wonder why there has been so much criticism. A good case in point may be that of Burundi refugees in Tanzania, on which at least four entire books have been written, all of them quite critical.[58] Liisa Malkki in a major study (very much inspired by the works of Mary Douglas)[59] thus compared the encamped refugees with another group who were roaming the streets of Tanzanian cities (the latter studied at length in a work by Marc Sommers) and found that it mainly served the goals of the host state which wanted to create 'a spatial order that would provide the basis for establishing other kinds of order (...). Thus, the spatial order was a necessary prerequisite for the "regularization" of their status and the "normalization" of their life.'[60] Referring to Michel Foucault, she also observed that

> In a refugee camp where people are contained for one overarching reason, their statelessness, the compartmentalization and regulation of space comes to have heightened practical and political significance. For there, normalization

DOI: 10.1057/9781137502797.0009

occurs first of all at the level of categories – most of all national categories. Just as it is unlikely that a zoo keeper would put creatures of different species in a single cage, so it seems to be standard practice that different national 'types' or 'kinds' are segregated as a matter of course in the administration of refugees. This practice is by now so standardized that it hardly ever seems to need rationalization.[61]

Simon Turner has offered a comparable analysis of life in another Tanzanian camp for Burundi refugees, Lukole. In his analysis, he is more inspired by Giorgio Agamben than Foucault, and he sees Lukole as 'an expression of Giorgio Agamben's camp as the hidden matrix and *nomos* of modern political space,' where the Foucauldian 'biopower is always underpinned by sovereign power,' approvingly quoting Agamben for his claim that 'the camp is the structure in which the state of exception is permanently realized' and referring for the latter concept to the Nazi political scientist Carl Schmitt:

> [T]he Tanzanian state decides that the refugees are a threat to the nation-state and puts them in this exceptional space, at once inside and outside the law, and the refugees are reduced to bare life, outside the polis of national citizens.[62]

For the sake of efficiency the camp was constructed to correspond to a 'bureaucratic grid,' but rather than a traditional Weberian ('rational-legal') state bureaucracy it was the humanitarian organisations, directed by the UNHCR, who were in charge of the exercise of a Foucauldian (albeit benevolent and caring) biopolitics,[63] thus seeking to transform the beneficiaries of their assistance into passive victims, but encountering resistance:

> [M]ost ground staff were generally committed to helping the refugees, but due to the bureaucratic imperative to count and control, a tug of war would often take place between relief staff and refugees. Relief staff would spend most of their time making rules and systems for ensuring that the refugees did not break them, while refugees would spend their time trying to bend the rules which they found unfair (...) Whereas most international staff were genuinely committed to aiding victims of war, they often found themselves wound up in bureaucratic logics over which they had no control.[64]

One of the consequences of the principled separation of humanitarianism from politics was for Agamben the denigration of refugees, especially in camps, from citizens without or outside their home country to pure victims, that is, zoë ('bare life') than bios, that is, full life

> The separation between humanitarianism and politics that we are experiencing today is the extreme phase of the separation of the rights of man

DOI: 10.1057/9781137502797.0009

from the rights of the citizen, in the final analysis, however, humanitarian organizations – which today are more and more supported by international commissions – can only grasp human life in the figure of bare or sacred life, and therefore, despite themselves, maintain a secret solidarity with the very powers they ought to fight. It takes only a glance at the recent publicity campaigns to gather funds for refugees from Rwanda to realize that here human life is exclusively considered (and there are certainly good reasons for this) as sacred life – which is to say, as life that can be killed but not sacrificed – and that only as such is it made into the object of aid and protection.[65]

Pretty much the same would appear to have all along been the case of the huge Dadaab camp complex established in northern Kenya for Somali refugees, many of which found themselves in a very protracted refugee situation. This has, among others, been described by Cindy Horst in her *Transnational Nomads*.[66] While agreeing with the aforementioned authors on the basics, she emphasises that the distinctions between 'vulnerable victims' and 'cunning crooks' do not do justice to the actual refugees with their 'fluid humanness'.[67] The standardised attitudes to the refugees, necessitated by the bureaucratic modus operandi tends to deprive them of agency and identity which even threatens making them 'Other to themselves'.[68] While acknowledging the risk of creating a 'refugee dependency syndrome,' the author nevertheless warns against this concept:

> NGO employees who believe in such a syndrome disregard the vulnerable position of a number of refugees, especially those who have to survive without economic and social capital. These employees diagnose the problem in the head of the refugees instead of in the structural position in which some refugees find themselves.[69]

The French anthropologist Michel Agier has an even more critical attitude towards the humanitarian organisations. Likewise, taking Foucault and Agamben as his theoretical points of departure he describes the refugees as 'the undesirables,' whose vulnerable position and treatment by the humanitarians reduce them to pure victims:

> Refugees are adopted by national and international NGOs and UN agencies in the name of human rights, and these take responsibility for them as pure victims, as if they owed their survival simply to the fact of no longer being present in the world, i.e. being de-socialized and in a state of purely biological life – a life that the representatives of the international community decide to extend rather than let extinguish. (...) To act and speak out in their places of exile means for the refugees rejecting the principle of their 'vulnerability' as justifying their treatment as nameless pure victims.[70]

DOI: 10.1057/9781137502797.0009

One of the problems with camp life, according to Agier, was similar to the absence of ordinary temporality mentioned earlier under concentration camps (vide supra).

> [T]he life of refugees and the situation of the camps are models of uncertainty. They are spaces and populations administered in the mode of emergency and exception, where time seems to have been stopped for an undetermined period. A camp is an emergency intervention that has been on 'stand-by' for months and years (...). Waiting becomes an eternity, an endless present (...) Waiting and absence thus may constitute the very essence of the present, a doubly painful one (...). The camp is a manifestation of an immediate present, since it excludes both past and future. It excludes them by excluding itself from all history, for past and present are only conceived, ultimately, in the Elsewhere of the lost land and the hypothetical future of return.[71]

Hence a lot of time is spent on recalling the past (which is usually a painful one) as a means of establishing a certain temporality, which may well lead to the creation of shared myths and to what the Somalis, according to Cindy Horst, call *Buufis*, a term with a rather indeterminate meaning, but which often includes 'hope, longing, desire or dream to go for resettlement,' a phenomenon similar to the various tales constructed by the encamped Burundi refugees in Tanzania described by Malkki, Turner and Sommers.[72]

Another Foucauldian disciple who is critical of the humanitarian approach to the refugee (especially asylum) question is Didier Fassin, who is also arguing against the 'victimisation' of refugees by humanitarians. This is, for instance, the case when (as happened in France) the right to asylum for political reasons is largely replaced by a granting of humanitarian residence permits based on medical needs.[73] Moreover, the personal accounts of the torture endured by many asylum seekers have been profoundly discredited in favour of medical certificates of the scars and other traces left on the body of the victim – a new 'regime of truth' which is all the more paradoxical, considering that new forms of torture are being invented which leave no bodily traces, but are no less painful for that.[74] Not only does this make little sense, but it also contributes to reducing the applicants to bodies, that is, Agambian 'bare life' or *zoē*, a move for which Fassin prefers the term 'politics of life' for the Foucauldian 'biopolitics.'[75]

Most camps have been designed with bureaucratic efficiency in mind,[76] that is, resembling military barracks more than ordinary villages or cities.

DOI: 10.1057/9781137502797.0009

In most camps, for both refugees and IDPs, forms of governance have to be established, as was the case for the ghettos and concentration camps of the past. While this may be a fairly unproblematic in some cases, in others – especially among the refugee warrior communities to which we shall return shortly – it means replicating the authority structures of the country of origin, which were responsible for the plight of the camp inmates and the main reason for their flight, as was to a large extent the case of (at least some of) the Cambodian camps in Thailand after the Vietnamese invasion in 1978, managed by the remnants of the Pol Pot regime, and the camps for the Rwandan Hutu refugees, which were run by the perpetrators of the 1994 genocide (vide infra).[77]

In some respects, the gender relations in the camps also replicated those of the country of origin, but in others this did not happen, as the men's role as breadwinners was often taken over by the humanitarian agencies, leaving the former *pater familias* almost emasculated, thereby producing all kinds of compensatory behaviour such as domestic violence and rape.[78] Occasionally, however, a flourishing business life developed in the camps, with camp inhabitants, both male and female, seeking supplementary earnings in the informal sector within or in the vicinity of the camps.[79]

5.5   Conflict and security aspects of refugees and their camps

Even though refugees are by definition victims, fleeing acute threats to their personal safety, that is, their 'human security,'[80] they may also constitute security threats to host countries.[81] At the very least, the influx of refugees into a country and the resultant presence of refugee camps on its territory may be discursively 'securitised' as convincingly argued in a work by Edward Mogire, focusing on two of Africa's most challenged host countries, Kenya and Tanzania.[82]

5.5.1   Securitising refugees

Securitisation merely requires a 'securitising actor' (often, but not necessarily, a government) to present a certain issue (e.g., that of refugees or migrants) as an 'existential' and urgent threat to a certain 'referent object' (often the state or nation, but sometimes other communities) and an audience (e.g., a parliament, electorate or any other community) willing

DOI: 10.1057/9781137502797.0009

to accept the gist of this 'speech act' or 'language game,' in which case it becomes possible to justify a resort to 'extraordinary measures.'[83]

In principle, any feature related to refugees may thus be securitised or 'desecuritised,' and there is neither a priori reason to expect the outcome of the competing discourses and counter-discourses (i.e., 'desecuritisation' attempts) to be permanent within a country nor identical between countries. There may nevertheless be some identifiable patterns. For instance, in countries experiencing severe environmental (or even climatic change-related) challenges such as drought or deforestation, it should come as no surprise if the use by refugees of scarce water or fire-wood might be securitised, as it seems to have been in connection with the Dadaab camp complex in eastern Kenya.[84] If refugees are forbidden to work or farm, then it is neither very surprising that some of them take to petty crime to make ends meet nor that this may be perceived as a serious security problem by the local population.[85] Similarly, in countries with contested national identities, perhaps based on 'delicate' ethnic balances, the very identity of the influx may be securitised, perhaps articulated as a challenge to the autochthonous parts of the population (i.e., the true 'sons of the soil') by *allochtons*, that is, 'strangers.'[86] Africa has, for instance, seen numerous instances of both centrally orchestrated and local and seemingly spontaneous outbreaks of violence against refugees qua strangers.[87]

The most serious problem may, however, be the link between armed conflict and refugees. Not only does armed conflict constitute one of the most common causes of refugee flows, but the causal arrow may also point in the opposite direction in the sense that refugees may also be at least one contributory cause of armed conflicts, albeit perhaps not so much by causing an outbreak of armed conflict as by spreading and intensifying such a conflict, to which problematic the following section is devoted.

5.5.2   Refugee (camp) militarisation

The fact that refugees (as well as IDPs) are treated by humanitarian agencies as passive victims and expected to behave accordingly has always entailed a profound paradox in view of what is required to meet the criteria of the 1951 convention, that is, to be at risk of persecution because of either political activities or *qua* belonging to a racial, ethnic or religious group or an undefined 'particular social group.'

These are all factors that are very often politicised – and the donor countries that are funding the humanitarian activities frequently demand

DOI: 10.1057/9781137502797.0009

the right to politicise them from the countries whence the refugees fled. To thus implicitly demand a person to have a direct or indirect political identity in order to be accepted as a refugee entitled to assistance, and then to expect him or her to immediately shed this identity upon joining the ranks of the refugees seems both illogical and unfair. While this seems to constitute a good reason for allowing political organisation and activities among refugees inside and outside of the camps, it may seem perfectly reasonable to demand that such political activities by refugees remain non-violent, for the sake of both other camp inmates and the host country and its citizens. Nevertheless, refugees in their camps have long been 'militarised,' and the trend would seem to be one of increasing militarisation in several respects.[88]

Some even refer to communities of 'refugee warriors,'[89] claiming that their presence in one country leads to a spread of civil war to neighbouring countries. There does indeed seem to be a statistically significant correlation between the two phenomena,[90] even though the direction of the 'arrow of causality' is more ambiguous: Do civil wars in a country lead to the formation of warrior refugee communities across the border, or does such a community create (or contribute to perpetuating) civil wars in neighbouring countries, or perhaps both?

We do not have to venture out into the Third World to find examples of at least plans for the deliberate recruitment of refugees as combatants. During the cold war, the Eisenhower administration thus made plans for a 'Volunteer Freedom Army' into which they envisioned to recruit refugees (or 'escapees') from the Communist countries in Europe. Even though it was never implemented, the idea was briefly reinvigorated during the Hungarian uprising in 1956.[91] One could also mention the ill-fated CIA-orchestrated Bay of Pigs invasion of Cuba in April 1961, in which Cuban exiles (i.e., refugees or escapees) in the United States served as proxies in what was in reality a US intervention;[92] or the so-called '*Contras*' comprising refugees from Nicaragua who were trained by the US to wage a guerrilla war against the leftist Sandinista regime in their home country.[93]

Palestinian refugee camps have also been very militarised, for example, in Jordan where their presence, and the fact that many of the inmates were armed militants, led to the 'Black September' offensive by means of which the Hashemite rulers of the country, including King Hussein, sought to eliminate what they saw (not entirely without reason) as a serious threat to their rule.[94] The armed Palestinian refugee population in

DOI: 10.1057/9781137502797.0009

Lebanon also represented a threat to this country's very fragile (partly consociationalist) power-sharing arrangement, and thus contributed to its temporary break-down in 1975/1976, and the ensuing civil war,[95] in addition to which many refugees joined the various liberation movements such as *Fatah*, PFLP (Popular Front for the Liberation of Palestine) and others.[96]

We have seen such refugee warriors in many civil wars around the world, as well as cases of genuine bona fide refugee communities which have been wrongfully accused of serving as warriors as an excuse for forcefully repatriating (or simply expelling) them, in reality for very different reasons. An example of the latter may have been the refugees in Lebanon, Jordan and Syria who had fled their native country, Iraq, which the US-led invasion in 2003 left in chaos and 'sectarian' civil war.[97] There are also examples of the presence of rebel organisations in refugee camps which does not lead to actual militarisation, as has (at least according to some analyses) been the case of the Karen refugees from Burma, residing in camps across the border in Thailand.[98] This lack of militarisation stood in sharp contrast to the former *Khmer Rouge* forces who had fled to Thailand after the 1978 Vietnamese invasion of 'Democratic Kampuchea' and who came to constitute a particularly nasty community of refugee warriors, who fought to depose the new Vietnam-supported government of Heng Samrin and re-install the mass murderous Pol Pot regime.[99] Their host country had been far less hospitable to the people (not least ethnic Vietnamese) who had fled from this regime and who subsequently played quite an active role in the Vietnamese invasion.[100]

Another refugee warrior community was that represented by Afghan refugees in Pakistan, fleeing the new communist rulers and their Soviet allies in the 1980s, out of which emerged the Taliban in the 1990s,[101] which continued to haunt the country until the present day. Africa has also seen more than its fair share of refugee warrior communities, which have often been catered for by the international humanitarian 'industry.' Examples include the ethnic Tigrayan refugees from Ethiopia with their organisation – as so often subdivided into a civilian and a military branch, the TPLF/A (Tigrayan People's Liberation Front/ Army).[102] The Eritrean refugees were mainly organised in the EPLF/A (Eritrean People's Liberation Front/Army) which had even established an Eritrean Relief Organization as its 'humanitarian' affiliate.[103] One could also mention the SPLM/A (Sudan People's Liberation Movement/ Army) which benefited immensely in their armed struggle (1983–2005)

DOI: 10.1057/9781137502797.0009

from international humanitarian relief (partly channelled through) an 'Operation Lifeline Sudan' (OLF) and who in 2011 formed the government of the new state of South Sudan, only to soon plunge the country into a new civil war.[104]

There are several other examples, of both militarisation and its absence, but let us stop here to review what the available evidence tells us about causality. In her excellent work *Dangerous Sanctuaries*, Sarah Lischer, seeks to determine why some refugee communities become militarised, but others not, inter alia by comparison along three dimensions.[105]

▸ Simultaneous refugee flows caused by the same emergency, but going in different directions, *in casu* from Afghanistan (after the Soviet invasion in 1979) to Pakistan and Iran, respectively, and from Burundi and Rwanda to Congo/Zaïre (*vide infra*) and to Tanzania, respectively, where those to Iran and Tanzania did not become significantly militarised, whereas those to Pakistan and the Congo did.[106]

▸ Three categories of refugees: 'Situational refugees' who are fleeing generalised insecurity and violence, 'persecuted refugees' who are fleeing more targeted threats based on their membership of particular groups, and what the author calls 'states-in-exile.' While situational refugees are rarely militarised (at least initially), whereas the persecuted ones often are, only surpassed by the states-in-exile refugees who are nearly always militarised. Moreover, whereas the former category usually repatriate voluntarily as soon as the security situation improves, persecuted refugees tend to require stronger guarantees and states-in-exile refugees tend to demand 'victory' before they repatriate.

▸ Two different ways of handling the influx of refugees, either separating the armed and militant ones from the unarmed civilians or refraining from this, be that due to a lack of will or ability. While Tanzania, for instance, to the best of its abilities sought to disarm the refugees, Zaïre did not, both because of a lack of will and capacity, whereas Pakistan did have the capacity, but lacked the will to disarm the Afghan refugees.

The significance of making such distinctions, difficult though they may be, is that it should allow for predicting whether the provision of humanitarian relief is likely to alleviate or aggravate an already very serious humanitarian emergency by, in the words of Lischer, 'feeding militants, sustaining and protecting militants' dependents, supporting a war

DOI: 10.1057/9781137502797.0009

economy, and providing legitimacy to combatants.'[107] The consequences thereof may be a prolongation and/or intensification of the armed struggle in the sending country, or a spread of the fighting to neighbouring countries.

A good example of situational refugees who are neither constituting a genuine security problem for the hosting country, nor have been securitised by it, and who voluntarily repatriated when the civil war in their home country came to an end, was the flow of around a million Mozambican refugees into neighbouring Malawi, fleeing a very bloody civil war between the ruling FRELIMO (*Frente de Libertação de Moçambique*: Front for the Liberation of Mozambique) and the rebel movement RENAMO (*Resistência Nacional Moçambicana*: Mozambican National Resistance) which was supported by first the racist Ian Smith regime in 'Rhodesia' and subsequently by the apartheid regime of South Africa.[108] The almost simultaneous refugee flow from the civil war in another former Portuguese colony, Angola, between the ruling MPLA (*Movimento Popular de Libertação de Angola*: Popular Liberation Movement of Angola) and the rebel group UNITA (*União Nacional para a Independência Total de Angola*: National Union for the Total Independence of Angola), however, was much more problematic. Most of the more than one million people displaced by the armed conflict remained within the borders of Angola as IDPs (usually referred to as *deslocados*, i.e., displaced), even though sizable contingents also went to Zaïre, Zambia and Namibia.[109]

One of the explanations was that the effect of the cold war on the two, otherwise quite similar, conflicts was different. While the USSR supported FRELIMO quite extensively, the US did not seriously become involved in support of its antagonists, whereas they did so in Angola in support of UNITA, along with such unlikely bed-fellows as Maoist China, Mobutu's Zaïre and apartheid South Africa, in response to which not only the Soviet Union, but also its ally (or proxy) Cuba provided massive support for the MPLA.[110] Another explanation was that the conflict resolution efforts and the subsequent deployment of peacekeeping missions were much more successful in Mozambique than in Angola.[111]

5.5.3   Case study: the Rwandan genocide and its regional reverberations

The worst-ever example of refugee militarisation is probably that of the refugees in Zaïre following the 1994 Rwandan genocide.[112]

DOI: 10.1057/9781137502797.0009

The background to this genocide also had quite a lot to do with refugees and forced displacement. In 1959, members of the Hutu majority group pre-empted the planned decolonisation by launching what they called a 'Hutu revolution,' essentially removing a large part of the hitherto privileged Tutsi elite from their positions of power. This was quite a brutal and bloody affair, sending a large part of the Tutsi into exile, mainly in Uganda but also in Tanzania and Zaïre. Especially in Uganda, the Rwandan refugees-turned-diaspora formed quite a cohesive and well-organised group, the military wing of which also undertook occasional military raids into their former home country.[113] Many of these provoked 'retaliatory' massacres by Hutu against local Tutsi, for example, the killing of approximately 10,000 civilian Tutsi in Rwanda in 'an orgy of violence' in 1963.[114] In the final years of Milton Obote's second presidentship most of them, organised in the Rwandan Patriotic Front/ Army (RPF/A) sided with the guerrilla forces of the present President Yoweri Museveni, the National Resistance Army (NRA), and after the latter's victory in 1986 some of them were even rewarded with appointments as officers in the new national army of Uganda.[115] After this rather short 'honeymoon,' however, the new Ugandan leader succumbed to popular pressure to repatriate the rather unpopular and unwelcome Rwandans, and Museveni now supported his former comrades-in-arms in a military quest for returning to their country of origin, commencing with a major 'invasion' in October 1990, which was soon repulsed, only to be succeeded by repeated and gradually more effective incursions.[116]

As the civil war came to look increasingly serious, the UN and various other external actors sought to broker a ceasefire, to be followed by a peace agreement, and in 1992 they managed to bring the parties together for negotiations in Arusha, Tanzania, where in August 1993 they finally signed the Arusha Agreement, stipulating a complex and multifaceted democracy-cum-power-sharing arrangement.[117] However, the 'internationalised civil war' had, ever since its beginning, been accompanied by preparations by Hutu extremists for a fully-fledged genocide of the Tutsi minority, which was launched within hours of a shoot-down of the presidential jet on the evening of 6 April 1994, commencing with killing squads apprehending and murdering their adversaries among the political elite, also including moderate Hutu, and proceeding to a full-scale slaughter of Tutsi throughout the country.[118]

In response, the RPA resumed its offensive whereby they not only managed to save a large number of Tutsi from extermination at the

DOI: 10.1057/9781137502797.0009

hands of the Hutu extremists, but also displaced a large number of Hutu civilians. Just as had some Tutsi fleeing from the genocide, some of the Hutu displaced by the RPA offensive found their way to Tanzania, where their arrival was mainly approached as an economic problem.[119] The bulk of both the consecutive outpourings of refugees, however, went west to neighbouring Zaïre, in what may well have been history's most massive flight,[120] comparable only to the refugee flows and death marches from the eastern front in the final months of WWII (*vide supra*).

Just as these westward death marches from the concentration camps had exhibited a blend of surviving victims (mainly Jews) and guilty-as-hell perpetrators such as their SS guards, the second Rwandan refugee flow also represented a curious mix of (more or less innocent[121]) civilians and genocidaires – and the final stages of it was facilitated by a UN-mandated 'humanitarian intervention' code-named *Operation Turquoise* launched by France as the loyal patron of the overthrown genocidal regime.[122] Neither the French troops deployed in Rwanda nor those of Zaïre across the border made any concerted efforts to separate civilians from members of the armed forces or genocidal militias such as the *Interahamwe*, or even to disarm the latter. As a result the former regime managed to transform the refugee camps in the Kivu provinces in Zaïre into miniature replicas of the Rwanda they had left, managed by the same local, provincial and national politicians and patrolled by armed genocidaires. Moreover, while they for a long time neglected the surviving IDPs in Rwanda, the international humanitarian agencies, including the UNHCR, catered quite generously for the refugees in the camps even though the former (interim) government had also emptied the state treasury and brought it along with them to the camps.[123]

Part of the explanation for the veritable congestion of the camps in the Kivu provinces with humanitarian agencies and non-governmental organisations (NGOs), including 'cowboy NGOs' with little or no experience or knowledge of local conditions,[124] was surely the growing 'marketisation' of humanitarian aid[125] and the unfortunate role of the media.[126] It simply mattered a lot to even the most respectable and well-intended humanitarian agencies to be not only present, but also visible, that is, in the spotlight of the media, and especially if their competitors were present lest the latter would get the next contract down the line. Needless to say, not everybody in the 'emergency relief industry' had exclusively unselfish motives, but even those who did were forced to play by the rules of the market. In recognition that something had

DOI: 10.1057/9781137502797.0009

gone terribly wrong with the Rwandan refugees, the Steering Committee for Humanitarian Response in late 1994 organised a meeting which produced a *Code of Conduct for the International Red Cross and Red Crescent Movement and Non-Governmental Organizations (NGOs) in Disaster Relief*, to which has later been added a peer review mechanism and a certification process, intended to regulate the less respectable organisations.[127]

The presence of genocidal 'refugee warriors' in the camps in Zaïre also made a spread of the conflict well-nigh inevitable.[128] Having regrouped into a new organisation, ALiR (*Armée pour la libération de Rwanda*: Army for the Liberation of Rwanda) later renamed FDLR (*Forces démocratiques de libération du Rwanda*: Democratic Forces for the Liberation of Rwanda)[129] they aligned themselves with the indigenous Mai-Mai group[130] and perpetrated several massacres of Congolese Tutsi of older 'vintage' Rwandan stock, including the so-called 'Banyamulenge,' in addition to which they launched raids into Rwanda, seemingly with the tacit approval of the long-standing Zairean dictator Mobutu.[131] Finding this intolerable, Rwanda (alongside Uganda) decided to overthrow the already moribund Mobutu regime, and (as a smoke-screen) helped form a resistance movement, the ADFL (*Alliance des Forces Démocratiques pour la Libération du Congo-Zaïre*: Alliance of Democratic Forces for the Liberation of Congo-Zaïre), partly consisting of refugees from Zaïre and headed by a former supporter of Congo's first prime minister, Patrice Lumumba, a Laurent Desiré Kabila of rather dubious repute.[132] Having successfully toppled Mobutu and replaced him with Kabila, Uganda and especially Rwanda proceeded to pursue the ALiR/FDLR and to forcefully repatriate the remaining Rwandan (Hutu) refugees in the country.[133]

Congo's new ruler soon tired of the massive presence of his former patrons and aligned himself with anti-Tutsi/Banyamulenge forces in the eastern part of the country, which provoked both Rwanda and Uganda to seek his overthrow, once again not only by creating an indigenous rebel group (the RCD: *Rassemblement Congolais pour la Démocratie*: Congolese Gathering for Democracy) to act on their behalf, but also by dispatching regular troops across the border in a fully-fledged military intervention. This in turn made Kabila (*Père*, soon to be assassinated and replaced by his son Joseph, known as Kabila *Fils*) ask the Congo's new formal allies in the Southern African Development Community (SADC) for assistance – a call to which three member states responded favourably, that is, Angola, Namibia and Zimbabwe. This turned the Congolese civil war into a highly internationalised affair, pitting four SADC member

DOI: 10.1057/9781137502797.0009

states against three foreign invaders, Rwanda, Uganda and Burundi.[134] Not only did the battle-lines thus become increasingly blurred (also because of the fall-out between the erstwhile allies Rwanda and Uganda producing as split of RCD into two opposing factions, RCD-Goma and RCD-Kisingani), but the initial motives of both the indigenous and the foreign actors also receded into the background in favour of economic motives, that is, the pillaging of the vast Congolese mineral resources.[135] This did not, unfortunately, limit the indiscriminate killing of civilians by all sides, according to some estimates bringing to total number of direct and indirect fatalities ('excess deaths') close to five million.[136]

In all stages of this extremely complex patchwork (or Gordian knot) of conflicts in Africa's Great Lake region have militarised refugees played important roles, as have indeed the humanitarians who have felt obliged to assist them.

5.5.4   'Sitting Ducks': refugees in camps and boats

Considering that refugee camps may be so militarised that they are seen as a threat to either the state where they are located or another state, typically the state of origin of the camp residents, it should not come as much of a surprise that they may come under attack. In quite a few cases, refugee camps, into which intended victims have been lured or forced, have thus been used as killing fields or veritable slaughter houses. Killing civilians in well-ordered and confined spaces such as a refugee (or IDP) camp is, after all, similar to 'shooting fish in a barrel.'

Apartheid South Africa thus on more than one occasion launched bombing raids against refugee camps in neighbouring countries such as Angola and Botswana believed to host ANC (African National Congress) militants.[137] In West Africa, Guinean refugee camps hosting refugees from both Liberia and Sierra Leone, similarly, came under military attack from both governments of the sending countries and rebel groups, just as the rebel group LURD (Liberians United for Reconciliation and Democracy) attacked Liberian refugees in Guinea in 2001 and 2002 with the approval of the government in Conakry.[138]

That such behaviour is not only encountered in Africa is obvious from the historical record. In 1982, following the forced evacuation of the PLO (Palestinian Liberation Organisation) from Lebanon in the wake of an Israeli invasion, armed members of a Christian Maronite militia, the Phalangists, were allowed by Israeli forces under the command of the late

DOI: 10.1057/9781137502797.0009

Ariel Sharon to enter the Palestinian refugee camps Sabra and Shatila, where they went on a veritable killing spree, murdering approximately 1,200 civilian Palestinians.[139]

In those cases where a refugee camp is host to parts of a refugee warrior community which launches attacks, perhaps limited to terrorist attacks, against either their country of origin or third parties, a legal case might even be made that an attack on such a camp would constitute self-defence and ipso facto be legal under international law, in some cases perhaps even to the point of an attack on the host state as such,[140] but whether such arguments would in fact convince the judges in a hypothetical war crimes case is far from certain.

Large columns of fleeing people, perhaps desperately trying to make their way from a battle field to the relative safety of a refugee camp, may be almost as tempting from a strictly military viewpoint, either because there may be grounds for suspecting enemy combatants of hiding among the civilians in flight, as the *genocidaires* from Rwanda did in the wake of the RPA's victorious offensive (*vide supra*), or because the civilians stand in the way of military operations. The latter seems, for instance, to have been the rationale for the notorious No Gun Ri massacre, perpetrated by the US forces against South Korean (*sic!*) refugees during the Korean War in the summer of 1950.[141]

Other refugees en route to presumed safety may be even more exposed than those travelling on foot, which is the case of 'boat people' finding themselves in terribly crammed conditions on-board usually small and primitive boats in international waters.[142] The world has witnessed this phenomenon in various places, including the following: In Southeast Asia the fall of Saigon in 1975 and the subsequent establishment of communist rule in what was previously South Vietnam produced a massive exodus of, first, the former regime and other members of the former elite as well as close collaborators with the US, most of whom were assisted in their flight (usually by air) and granted asylum almost automatically. This first wave was, however, followed by the gradual and much less centrally controlled exodus of ordinary civilians, usually in small boats heading for neighbouring countries such as Thailand, where this influx of boat people was not exactly welcomed.[143] It seems that Bangkok unofficially condoned and appreciated the wave of piratical attacks against the refugee-carrying boats, featuring the plundering, abuse and frequent rape of their passengers who were then often thrown overboard to perish in the shark-infested waters.[144] More recently, there

DOI: 10.1057/9781137502797.0009

have been waves of persecuted (almost exclusively Muslim) Rohingyans fleeing ethnic and religious persecution in Burma, who have also faced hardships en route and been less than welcome in their countries of refuge.[145]

Australia had been the recipient of thousands of boat people through the 1960s, 1970s and 1980s, for example, from East Timor following the Indonesian occupation in 1976.[146] From the 1990s, however, the country became significantly less hospitable and in 2000, for instance, made an agreement with Indonesia about detaining refugees en route to Australia.[147] In 2001 the government in Canberra earned itself international notoriety by ordering the forceful diversion and subsequent boarding of the Norwegian freighter MV *Tampa* which had responded to an Australian vessel-in-distress call from a stranded fishing boat (*Palapa-1*) carrying more than 400 boat people. As Australia refused access to its off-shore territory, the Christmas Island, it all ended up with the survivors being brought to the small island state of Nauru.[148] Not only does such behaviour seem to violate universal humanitarian norms as well as, in some cases, national legislation, but it may also constitute a breach of several binding maritime conventions.[149]

In the wake of 9/11, the attitude to boat people seems to have become even more hostile, even though arrival as a 'boat person' would seem to be one of the least likely routes into Australia for a prospective terrorist. Indeed, it would be a lot easier to just apply for a tourist visa.[150] One might perhaps have expected the US to take kindly to boat people, considering that some of the very first immigrants to what is today the USA were arguably boat people, that is, the 102 passengers on-board the good ship the *Mayflower* in 1620, whose trans-Atlantic voyage was motivated by their well-founded fear of persecution in Europe on the basis of their religious beliefs, most of them being Puritans.[151] However, the US attitude to contemporary boat people has not been particularly friendly. The Caribbean Ocean and adjacent seas such as the Gulf of Mexico and the Florida Straits have seen several waves of refugees, mainly from Cuba and Haiti to the US. The first waves of Cuban refugees were generally assisted and helped, even as far as their flight itself was concerned, because they were seen as either freedom fighters or at least as living testimonies of the human rights violations of their communist country of origin. There were, however, problems with integrating the influx into the local communities and detrimental effects on the labour market in

DOI: 10.1057/9781137502797.0009

Florida, especially in connection with the great Mariel boatlift of 1980,[152] which led to suspicions that the Castro regime deliberately created a new crisis (the 'Balseros Crisis') in 1994 in order to put pressure on Washington.[153]

The refugees from Haiti were even less welcome, including those who were clearly fleeing personal persecution, because their persecutors were US cold war allies such as the two generations of Duvaliér dictators, better known as Papa and Baby Doc, respectively, of whom the former ruled from 1957 to 1986 and the latter most of the time between 1991 and 2004.[154] The policy was initially to intern most of the refugees from the military coup in 1991 at Guantanamo, and in 1992, Washington even switched to a policy of maritime interception of boats and *refoulement* to Haiti of their passengers.[155]

While most of the Somali refugees have gone to Kenya and Ethiopia, some had fled to Yemen on the other side of the Gulf of Aden. Although their reception in Yemen has generally not been too bad, and the journey usually quite short, it has often been quite perilous and often taken the form of a human trafficking by unscrupulous criminal gangs.[156]

Even though the European countries tend to see themselves as generous and law-abiding states *Rechtsstaaten*, their attitudes – also reflected in the EU to which most of them belong – reveal themselves as far less generous, typically by granting asylum on the basis of a 'due process' treatment of applications for it, but making it as difficult as possible to actually file such an application.[157] In this respect boat people present special problems, mainly because they transit from the territory of the country of origin (or a transit country) through international waters where they cannot remain indefinitely. Even though one might, in principle, envision waves of boat people in the Baltic, North Sea or English Channel, they have not materialised, but the problem has only emerged in the Mediterranean and Adriatic seas as well as in the Canary Islands in the Atlantic Ocean, the recipient countries being Italy, Greece, Spain and Malta as well as, to a much lesser extent, France.

Italy first experienced several waves of seaborne refugees as well as irregular migrants from Albania, some of whom fled persecution, thus meeting the criteria for refugee status, while others did not, as they were fleeing for socio-economic reasons such as the collapse of the bizarre 'pyramid schemes' and the country's generally chaotic situation in the 1990s.[158] Then came waves of refugees from (or via)

DOI: 10.1057/9781137502797.0009

North Africa towards Europe where most landed in Italy, often at the island of Lampedusa.[159] Most recently Italy has been the recipient of a large number of bona fide refugees, who were fleeing persecution or general violence in connection with the 'Arab Spring' featuring large-scale emergencies such as the Libyan and Syrian civil wars.[160] Malta has also received far more than its fair share of boat people,[161] as has Spain, particularly as far as its off-shore possessions, the Canary Islands, are concerned.[162]

Rather than accepting what would appear to be its reasonable collective share of the global refugee population and then sharing the burden among the individual countries, Europe (especially the EU) has adopted the much more ethically dubious policy of seeking to minimise the total influx of refugees and other migrants and then refusing an equitable intra-European burden-sharing. The latter objective is achieved via the aforementioned 'Dublin procedure' while the former has been pursued via maritime interdiction (e.g., implemented via FRONTEX, that is, the European Agency for the Management of Operational Cooperation at the External Borders of the Member States of the European Union),[163] extra-territorial processing of asylum claims[164] and various collaboration agreements with countries on the southern littoral of the Mediterranean Sea.

5.6   Summary

The rather elaborate account above has clearly shown that there are many different links between 'people in flight' and encampment.

It even seems likely that the two main alternatives to refugee camps, repatriation and the granting of asylum, will continue their present decline as a result of two developments: On the one hand, the conflicts and other calamities in countries of origin are becoming more protracted, thus ruling out the fast repatriation that used to be the general rule. On the other hand, the willingness of host countries to accept refugees by granting them asylum will continue its present decline, especially in the countries of the global North who are in a much better position to host the refugees than the next door neighbouring countries where the refugees first seek shelter and protection. Thus caught between the proverbial rock and a hard place, growing numbers of people in flight will thus have few alternatives to accepting protracted sojourns in refugee camps with

DOI: 10.1057/9781137502797.0009

the benefits in the sense of 'beds for the night' and so on, and the costs in terms of dependency syndromes and loss of dignity.

It does not help at all that the arrival of refugees is increasingly being securitised, either through more concrete allegations that the people knocking on the European and North American doors are in reality prospective terrorists or criminals, or through more vague references to threats to national identities, usually premised on a lumping together of refugees and ordinary migrants. Nor does it help those standing up for more forthcoming attitudes that there are small grains of truth in such securitisation narratives, that is, a few people arriving for economic motives, but claiming to be fleeing persecution; or even fewer asylum seekers driven by more nefarious motives, such as finding more profitable loci for criminal activities than their countries of origin or even the wish to destroy western societies, for example, by means of terrorism.

In some cases, securitisation may thus be justified, for example, when it comes to 'refugee warriors' of which quite a few examples have been mentioned earlier, most evidently the Rwandan genocidaires in the present DR Congo. In such cases, remedial action against them, if need be by military means, may even be justified for states with the primary responsibility of their own citizens. The obvious solution ex ante is to ensure the disarmament of the arrivals to a refugee camp and a separation of combatants from civilians, but if this has been neglected a case could surely be made for an ex post forceful demilitarisation of the camps.

Notes

1   P. Marfleet (2006) *Refugees in the Global Era* (Houndmills: Palgrave Macmillan), 57–140.
2   J.M. Hintermaier (2000) 'The First Modern Refugees? Charity, Entitlement and Persuasion in the Huguenot Migration of the 1680,' *Albion*, 32:3, 429–449; R.D. Gwynn (1983) 'The Number of Huguenot Immigrants in England in the Late Seventeenth Century,' *Journal of Historical Geography*, 9:4, 384–395.
3   A.G. Oden (2001) *And You Welcomed Me: A Sourcebook on Hospitality in Early Christianity* (Nashville, TN: Abingdon Press); C.D. Pohl (2006) 'Responding to Strangers: Insights from the Christian Tradition,' *Studies in Christian Ethics*, 19:1, 81–101.

DOI: 10.1057/9781137502797.0009

4   D. Christiansen (1996) 'Movement, Asylum, Borders: Christian Perspectives', *International Migration Review*, 30:1, 7–17; L. Bretherton (2006) 'The Duty of Care to Refugees, Christian Cosmopolitanism, and the Hallowing of Bare Life', *Studies in Christian Ethics*, 19:1, 39–61.

5   Pius XII (1952) 'Exsul Familia Nazarethana', *Papal Encyclicals Online*, www. papalencyclicals.net/Pius12/ p12exsul.htm.

6   S.N. Agha (2008) 'The Ethics of Asylum in Early Muslim Society', *Refugee Survey Quarterly*, 27:2, 30–40; K. Elmadmad (2008) 'Asylum in Islam and in Modern Refugee Law', ibid., 51–63; A. Abou-El-Wafa (2009) *The Right to Asylum between Islamic Shari'ah and International Refugee Law: A Comparative Study* (Riyad: UNHCR Regional Office).

7   A. Betts et al. (2012) *UNHCR: The Politics and Practice of Refugee Protection*. 2nd ed. (London: Routledge), 7–17; E. Haddad (2008) *The Refugee in International Society: Between Sovereigns* (Cambridge: Cambridge University Press), 99–127.

8   V. Chetail (2003) 'Fridtjof Nansen and the International Protection of Refugees: An Introduction', *Refugee Survey Quarterly*, 22:1, 1–6; I.C. Jackson (2003) 'Dr. Fridtjof Nansen: A Pioneer in the International Protection of Refugees', ibid., 7–20; O. Hieronymi (2003) 'The Nansen Passport: A Tool of Freedom of Movement and of Protection', ibid., 36–47; A. Roversi (2003) 'The Evolution of the Refugee Regime and Institutional Responses: Legacies from the Nansen Period', ibid., 21–34.

9   K. Long (2009) 'Early Repatriation Policy: Russian Refugee Return 1922–1924', *Journal of Refugee Studies*, 22:2, 133–154.

10 L.W. Holborn (1938) 'The Legal Status of Political Refugees, 1920–1938', *American Journal of International Law*, 32:4, 680–703; D. Chatty (2013) 'Refugees, Exiles, and Other Forced Migrants in the Late Ottoman Empire', *Refugee Survey Quarterly*, 32:2, 35–52.

11 T.P. Maga (1982) 'Closing the Door: The French Government and Refugee Policy, 1933–1939', *French Historical Studies*, 12:3, 424–442; R.J. Beck (1999) 'Britain and the 1933 Refugee Convention: National or State Sovereignty?' *International Journal of Refugee Law*, 11:4, 597–624.

12 L.W. Holborn (1956) *The International Refugee Organization: A Specialized Agency of the United Nations, Its History and Work, 1946–1952* (Oxford: Oxford University Press).

13 G. Loescher (2002) *The UNHCR and World Politics: A Perilous Path* (Oxford: Oxford University Press, 2002), passim; idem and J. Millner (2011) 'UNHCR and the Global Governance of Refugees', in A. Betts (ed.) *Global Migration Governance* (Oxford: Oxford University Press), 189–209.

14 P. Weis (1967) 'The 1967 Protocol Relating to the Status of Refugees and Some Questions of the Law of Treaties', *British Yearbook of International Law*, 42, 39–70; S.E. Davies (2007) 'Redundant or Essential? How Politics Shaped

the Outcome of the 1967 Protocol, *International Journal of Refugee Law*, 19:4, 703–728.

15   A. Betts (2009) *Protection by Persuasion: International Cooperation in the Refugee Regime* (Ithaca, NY: Cornell University Press); idem (2009) *Forced Migration and Global Politics* (Oxford: Wiley-Blackwell); L. Barnett (2002) 'Global Governance and the Evolution of the International Refugee Regime,' *International Journal of Refugee Law*, 14:2, 238–262; J. Mertus (1998) 'The State and the Post-Cold War Refugee Regime: New Models, New Questions,' ibid., 10:3, 321–348; C.B. Keely (2001) 'The International Refugee Regime(s): The End of the Cold War Matters,' *International Migration Review*, 35:1, 303–314; B.S. Chimmi (2001) 'Reforming the International Refugee Regime: A Dialogic Model,' *Journal of Refugee Studies*, 14:2, 151–168; G. Scalettaris (2007) 'Refugee Studies and the International Refugee Regime: A Reflection on a Desirable Separation,' *Refugee Survey Quarterly*, 26:3, 36–50.

16   Its mandate was set out in *UN Documents*, A/RES/302, and its website is found at www.unrwa.org/. See also W. Dale (1974) 'UNRWA: A Subsidiarity Organ of the United Nations,' *International and Comparative Law Quarterly*, 23:3, 576–609; R. Bocco (2008) 'UNRWA and the Palestinian Refugees: A History within History,' *Refugee Survey Quarterly*, 28:2–3, 229–252; J. Al-Husseini (2000) 'UNRWA and the Palestinian Nation-Building Process,' *Journal of Palestinian Studies*, 29:2, 51–64.

17   E. Arboleda (1991) 'Refugee Definition in Africa and Latin America: The Lessons of Pragmatism,' *International Journal of Refugee Law*, 3:2, 185–207; G. Okoth-Obbo (2001) 'Thirty Years on: A Legal Review of the 1969 OAU Refugee Convention Governing the Specific Aspects of Refugee Problems in Africa,' *Refugee Survey Quarterly*, 20:1, 79–138; M.B. Rankin (2005) 'Extending the Limits or Narrowing the Scope? Deconstructing the OAU Refugee Definition Thirty Years On,' *South African Journal on Human Rights*, 21:3, 406–435.

18   For the Spanish text see www.unhcr.org/45dc19084.html. See aso R. Cuéllar et al. (1991) 'Refugee and Related Developments in Latin America: Challenges Ahead,' *International Journal of Refugee Law*, 3:3, 482–498.

19   J. Allain (2001) 'The *Jus Cogens* Nature of *Non-Refoulement*,' *International Journal of Refugee Law*, 13:4, 533–558; A. Duffy (2008) 'Expulsion to Face Torture? *Non-Refoulement* in International Law,' ibid., 20:3, 373–390; G.S. Goodwin-Gill (2011) 'The Right to Seek Asylum: Interception at Sea and the Principle of Non-Refoulement,' ibid., 23:3, 433–457; J. Durieux and J. MacAdams (2004) '*Non-Refoulement* through Time: The Case for a Derogation Clause to the Refugee Convention in Mass Influx Emergencies,' ibid., 16:1, 4–24.

20   *Convention Relating to the Status of Stateless Persons*, at www.unhcr. org/3bbb25729.html; *Convention on the Reduction of Statelessness*, at http://

DOI: 10.1057/9781137502797.0009

legal.un.org/ilc/texts/instruments/english/conventions/6_1_1961.pdf. See also C.A. Batchelor (1995) 'Stateless Persons: Some Gaps in International Protection,' *International Journal of Refugee Law*, 7:2, 232–259; idem (2006) 'Transforming International Legal Principles into National Law: The Right to a Nationality and the Avoidance of Statelessness,' *Refugee Survey Quarterly*, 25:3, 8–25; J.L. Blackman (1998) 'State Succession and Statelessness: The Emerging Right to an Effective Nationality under International Law,' *Michigan Journal of International Law*, 19:4, 1141–1194; D. Weissbrodt and C. Collins (2006) 'The Human Rights of Stateless Persons,' *Human Rights Quarterly*, 28:1, 245–276.

21   Most of the relevant legal documents are included in United Nations High Commissioner for Human Rights, OHCHR (2002) *Human Rights: A Compilation of International Instruments*. I. *Universal Instruments* (New York: United Nations).

22   J.L. Black-Branch (1996) 'Observing and Enforcing Human Rights under the Council of Europe: The Creation of a Permanent European Court of Human Rights,' *Buffalo Journal of International Law*, 3:1, 1–32; A. Drzemczewski (1998) 'The European Human Rights Convention: A New Court of Human Rights in Strasbourg as of November 1, 1998,' *Washington and Lee Law Review*, 55:4, 697–736.

23   This is known as the 'Sufi and Elmi v. the United Kingdom' case, on which see Council of Europe (2013) *Handbook on European Law Relating to Asylum, Borders and Immigration*, 69. See also H. Lambert (2013) 'The Next Frontier: Expanding Protection in Europe for Victims of Armed Conflict and Indiscriminate Violence,' *International Journal of Refugee Law*, 25:2, 207–234; H. Storey (2012) 'Armed Conflict in Asylum Law: The "War Flaw",' *Refugee Survey Quarterly*, 31:2, 1–32.

24   See Human Rights Watch (2013). *World Report 2013* (New York: HRW), 430–432, 434–435, 438–439. On Greece the verdict of the European Court of Human Rights in the *Case of M.S.S. v. Belgium and Greece*, Application no. 30696/09 (Strasbourg 9 January 2011), especially 30–40. On this case see also V. Moreno-Lax (2012) 'Dismantling the Dublin System: M.S.S. v. Belgium and Greece,' *European Journal of Migration and Law*, 14:1, 1–31. On Greece see also P.N. Papadimitrou and I. Papageorgiou (2005) 'The New "Dubliners": Implementation of European Council Regulation 343/2003 (Dublin II) by Greek Authorities,' *Journal of Refugee Studies*, 18:3, 299–318; K. Rozakou (2012) 'The Biopolitics of Hospitality in Greece: Humanitarianism and the Management of Refugees,' *American Ethnologist*, 39:3, 562–577; P. McDonough and E. Tsourdi (2012) 'The "Other" Greek Crisis: Asylum and EU Solidarity,' *Refugee Survey Quarterly*, 31:4, 67–100.

25   E. Thielemann (2003) 'Between Interests and Norms: Explaining Burden-sharing in the European Union,' *Journal of Refugee Studies*, 16:3, 253–273; idem and C. Armstrong (2013) 'Understanding European

Asylum Cooperation under the Schengen/Dublin System: A Public
Goods Framework,' *European Security*, 22:2, 148–164; S. Velluti (2014)
*Reforming the Common European Asylum System: Legislative Developments
and Judicial Activism* (Heidelberg: Springer); H. Gray (2013) 'Surveying
the Foundations: Article 80 TFEU and the Common European Asylum
System,' *Liverpool Law Review*, 34:2, 175–193; I. Staffans (2010) 'Judicial
Protection and the New European Asylum Regime,' *European Journal of
Migration and Law*, 12:2, 273–297; F. Comte (2010) 'A New Agency Is Born in
the European Union: The European Asylum Support Office,' ibid., 373–405;
F. Ippolito and S. Velluti (2011) 'The Recast Process of the EU Asylum
System: A Balancing Act between Efficiency and Fairness,' *Refugee Survey
Quarterly*, 30:3, 24–62.

26 I. Glynn (2011) 'The Genesis and Development of Article 1 of the 1951
Refugee Convention,' *Journal of Refugee Studies*, 25:1, 134–148.

27 In 2008 the UNHCR acknowledged the issue by adopting the 'UNHCR
Guidance Note on Refugee Claims Relating to Sexual Orientation and
Gender Identity'. For a critique see N. La Violette (2010) 'UNHCR Guidance
Note on Refugee Claims Relating to Sexual Orientation and Gender Identity:
A Critical Commentary,' *International Journal of Refugee Law*, 22:2, 173–208.
It has now been replaced by 'Guidelines on International Protection no.
9: Claims to Refugee Status Based on Sexual Orientation and/or Gender
Identity within the Context of Article 1A(2) of the 1951 Convention and/or its
1967 Protocol Relating to the Status of Refugees,' now referring to LGBTI, the
last letter standing for 'Intersex,' and available at www.unhcr.org/50ae466f9.
html.

28 N. Valji (2001) 'Women and the 1951 Refugee Convention: Fifty Years of
Seeking Visibility,' *Refuge*, 19:5, 25–35; S. Siddiqui (2010) 'Membership in a
Particular Social Group: All Approaches Open Doors for Women to Qualify,'
Arizona Law Review, 52:2, 505–532.

29 S. Williams (2005) 'Genocide: The Cambodian Experience,' *International
Criminal Law Review*, 5:3, 447–462; B. Kiernan (2007) *Blood and Soil: A World
History of Genocide and Extermination from Sparta to Darfur* (New Haven, CT:
Yale University Press), 539–554; idem (2008) *The Pol Pot Regime: Race, Power,
and Genocide in Cambodia under the Khmer Rouge, 1975–79*. 3rd ed. (New
Haven, CT: Yale University Press). For an elaborate, but not really convincing
argument that the bulk of the killing was genocidal see H. Hannum (1989)
'International Law and Cambodian Genocide: The Sounds of Silence,' *Human
Rights Quarterly*, 11:1, 82–138.

30 Figures from UNHCR: *Syrian Regional Refugee Response* at http://data.unhcr.
org/syrianrefugees/ regional.php, accessed 12 September 2014.

31 M.E. Price (2009) *Rethinking Asylum: History, Purpose, and Limits* (Cambridge:
Cambridge University Press), 69–72. On various religious norms pertaining

DOI: 10.1057/9781137502797.0009

to asylum see P. Marfleet (2011) 'Understanding "Sanctuary": Faith and Traditions of Asylum,' *Journal of Refugee Studies*, 24:3, 440–455.

32 S.L. Carruthers (2005) 'Between Camps: Eastern Block "Escapees" and Cold War Borderlands,' *American Quarterly*, 57:3, 911–942; G. Ginsburgs (1957) 'The Soviet Union and the Problems of Refugees and Displaced Persons, 1917–1956,' *American Journal of International Law*, 51:2, 325–361; Marfleet, *Refugees in the Global Era* (n. 1), 146–150.

33 K. Lowe (2013) *Savage Continent: Europe in the Aftermath of World War II* (London: Penguin), 27–34; A-M. de Zayas (2006). *A Terrible Revenge: The Ethnic Cleansing of the East European Germans*. 2nd ed. (New York: Palgrave Macmillan); N.M. Naimark (2001) *Fires of Hatred: Ethnic Cleansing in Twentieth-Century Europe* (Cambridge, MA: Harvard University Press), 108–130; U. Merten (2012) *Forgotten Voices: The Expulsion of Germans from Eastern Europe after World War II* (New Brunswick, NJ: Transaction Publishers).

34 K. O'Burne (2013) 'Is There a Need for Better Supervision of the Refugee Convention?' *Journal of Refugee Studies*, 26:3, 330–359; J. Whiteman and C. Nielsen (2013) 'Lessons from Supervisory Mechanisms in International and Regional Law,' ibid., 360–392; A. Blackham (2013) 'A Proposal for Enhanced Supervision of the Refugee Convention,' ibid., 392–415.

35 B. Brecht (1967) 'Gedanken über die Dauer des Exils,' from idem 'Svendborger Gedichte,' in idem: *Gesammelte Werke*, 9 (Frankfurt a.M.: Suhrkamp Verlag), 719–720. Translation by the author.

36 G. Loescher and J. Milner (2005) 'Protracted Refugee Situations: Domestic and International Security Implications,' *Adelphi Papers*, 375; idem and idem (2004) 'Protracted Refugee Situations and State and Regional Insecurity,' *Journal of Conflict and Security Law*, 4:1, 3–20; idem, idem, E. Newman and G. Troeller (2007) 'Protracted Refugee Situations and the Regional Dynamics of Peacebuilding,' ibid., 7:3, 491–501; K. Derouen, Jr. and M. Barutciski (2007) 'The Link Between Protracted Refugee Situations and Civil War in Africa: Encouraging New Direction for Research,' *Civil Wars*, 9:2, 214–225.

37 For a number of case studies G. Loescher et al., eds. (2008) *Protracted Refugee Situations: Poitical, Human Rights and Security Implications* (Tokyo: United Nations University Press); H. Adelman, ed. (2008) *Protracted Displacement in Asia: No Place to Call Home* (Aldershot: Ashgate).

38 F.M. Deng (1993) *Protecting the Dispossessed: A Challenge for the International Community* (Washington, DC: Brookings Institution); R. Cohen and F.M. idem (1998) *Masses in Flight: The Global Crisis of Internal Displacement* (Washington, DC: Brookings Institution); idem and idem, eds. (1998) *The Forsaken People: Case Studies of the Internally Displaced* (Washington, DC: Brookings Institution); M. Vincent and B.R. Sorensen, eds. (2001) *Caught*

DOI: 10.1057/9781137502797.0009

between Borders: Response Strategies of the Internally Displaced (London: Pluto Press).

39   F.M. Deng et al. (1996) *Sovereignty as Responsibility: Conflict Management in Africa* (Washington, DC: Brookings Institution), 32. For an account of the gradual acceptance of these principles in Africa see F.M. Deng and I.W. Zartman (2002) *A Strategic Vision for Africa: The Kampala Movement* (Washington, DC: Brookings Institution).

40   International Commission on Intervention and State Sovereignty, ICISS (2001) *The Responbsibility to Protect: Report of the International Commission on Intervention and State Sovereignty* (Ottawa: International Development Research Centre); A.J. Bellamy (2009) *Responsibility to Protect: The Global Effort to End Mass Atrocities* (Cambridge: Polity Press), 35–97; idem (2011) *Global Responsibility to Protect: From Words to Deeds* (London: Routledge); T.G. Weiss (2007) *Humanitarian Intervention: Ideas in Action* (Cambridge: Polity Press), 88–118; G. Evans (2008) *The Responsibility to Protect: Ending Mass Atrocity Crimes Once and For All* (Washington, DC: Brookings Institution), 31–54; A. Orford (2011) *International Authority and the Responsibility to Protect* (Cambridge: Cambridge University Press); A. Hehir (2012) *The Responsibility to Protect: Rhetoric, Reality and the Future of Humanitarian Intervention* (Houndmills: Palgrave Macmillan). The present author is also writing a work (in two volumes) on the topic, which is expected to be out in 2015/16.

41   T.G. Weiss and D.A. Korn (2006) *Internal Displacement: Conceptualization and Its Consequences* (London: Routledge).

42   *Guiding Principles on Internal Displacement*, Introduction, §2 in Internal Displacement Monitoring Centre: 'The Definition of an Internally Displaced Person (IDP)', at www.internal-displacement.org/.

43   'African Union Convention for the Protection and Assistance of Internally Displaced Persons in Africa', available at www.internal-displacement.org/. See also S. Ojeda (2010) 'The Kampala Convention on Internally Displaced Persons: Some International Humanitarian Law Perspectives', *Refugee Survey Quarterly*, 29:3, 58–66; A.M. Abebe (2010) 'The African Union Convention on Internally Displaced Persons: Its Codification Background, Scope, and Enforcement Challenges', ibid., 28–57; F. Guistiniani (2010) 'New Hopes and Challenges for the Protection of IDPs in Africa: The Kampala Convention for the Protection and Assistance of Internally Displaced Persons in Africa', *Denver Journal of International Law and Policy*, 39:2, 347–370.

44   P.D. Williams (2007) 'From Non-Intervention to Non-Indifference: The Origins and Developments of the African Union's Security Culture', *African Affairs*, 106:423, 253–279; idem (2009) 'The "Responsibility to Protect", Norm Localisation, and African International Society', *Global Responsibility to Protect*, 1:3, 392–416; K. Aningi and S. Atuobi (2009) 'Responsibility to

DOI: 10.1057/9781137502797.0009

Protect in Africa: An Analysis of the African Union's Peace and Security Architecture,' ibid., 90–113.

45   Both the 1966 human rights covenants and the Universal Declaration of Human Rights of 1948, on which they are grounded, are included in OHCHR, *Human Rights* (n. 21), 1–34.

46   P. Penz (2006) 'Displacement by Development and Moral Responsibility: A Theoretical Treatment,' in F. Crépau et al. eds. (2006) *Forced Displacement and Global Processes: A View from Forced Migration Studies* (Lanham, MD: Lexington Books), 63–89; idem et al. (2011) *Displacement by Development: Ethics, Rights and Responsibilities* (Cambridge: Cambridge University Press).

47   M. Dowie (2011) *Conservation Refugees: The Hundred-Year Conflict between Global Conservation and Native Peoples* (Cambridge, MA: MIT Press).

48   J. McAdam, ed. (2012) *Climate Change and Displacement: Multidisciplinary Perspectives* (Oxford: Hart Publishing); L. Scott et al., eds. (2012) *Climate Change and Displacement Reader* (London: Routledge).

49   S. Long and J. Wormworth (2012) 'Tuvalu: Islanders Lose Ground to Rising Seas,' in Scott et al. *Climate Change* (n. 48), 399–404; I. Kelman (2012) 'Island Evacuation,' ibid., 405–407.

50   J. McAdam (2012) '"Disappearing States", Statelessness and the Boundaries of International Law,' in Scott et al. *Climate Change* (n. 48), 105–129.

51   T.G. Rosenmeyer (1956) 'Plato's Atlantis Myth: "Timaeus" or "Critias"?' *Phoenix*, 10:4, 163–172; S. Dusanic (1982) 'Plato's Atlantis,' *L'Antiquité Classique*, 51, 25–52.

52   N. Van Hear (2006) Nicholas: '"I Went as Far as My Money Would Take Me": Conflict, Forced Migration and Class,' in Crépau et al. eds. *Forced Displacement* (n. 46), 125–157.

53   IDMC (2013) *Global Overview 2012: People Internally Displaced by Conflict and Violence* (Geneva: IDMC).

54   M. Tessler (1994) *A History of the Israeli-Palestinian Conflict* (Bloomington, IN: Indiana University Press), 273–335; Y. Sayigh (1997) *Armed Struggle and the Search for State: The Palestinian National Movement, 1949–1993* (Oxford: Clarendon Press), 35–58; R. Khalidi (1997) *Palestinian Identity: The Construction of Modern National Consciousness* (New York: Columbia University Press).

55   UNRWA (2012) *About UNRWA* (Jerusalem: UNRWA); R.G. Khouri (2010) 'Sixty Years of UNRWA: From Service Provision to Refugee Protection,' *Refugee Survey Quarterly*, 28:2–3, 438–451; H. Rueff and A. Viaro (2010) 'Palestinian Refugee Camps: From Shelter to Habitat,' ibid., 339–359; M. Kagan (2010) 'Is There Really a Protection Gap? UNRWA's Role Vis-á-Vis Palestinian Refugees,' ibid., 511–530.

56   'UNRWA in Figures as of 1 January 2013' at www.unrwa.org/sites/default/files/2013042435340.pdf.

DOI: 10.1057/9781137502797.0009

57 See, for instance, B. Harrell-Bond and E. Voutira (1992) 'Anthropology and the Study of Refugees', *Anthropology Today*, 8:4, 6–10; idem and idem (2007) 'In Search of "Invisible" Actors: Barriers to Access in Refugee Research', *Journal of Refugee Studies*, 20:2, 281–298; S.R. Waldron (1988) 'Working in the Dark: Why Social Anthropological Research Is Essential in Refugee Administration', ibid., 1:2, 153–165; E. Colson (2003) 'Forced Migration and the Anthropological Response', ibid., 16:1, 1–18; M. Eastmond (2007) 'Stories as Lived Experience: Narratives in Forced Migration Research', ibid., 20:2, 248–264.

58 L.H. Malkki (1995) *Purity and Exile: Violence, Memory, and National Cosmology among Hutu Refugees in Tanzania* (Chicago, IL: Chicago University Press); M. Sommers (2001) *Fear in Bongoland: Burundi Refugees in Urban Tanzania* (Oxford: Berghahn Books); P.O. Daley (2007) *Gender and Genocide in Burundi: The Search for Peace in the Great Lakes Region* (Oxford: James Currey); S. Turner (2010) *Politics of Innocence: Hutu Identity, Conflict and Camp Life* (Oxford: Berghahn Books).

59 M. Douglas (1966) *Purity and Danger: An Analysis of the Concepts of Pollution and Taboo* (London: Routledge and Kegan Paul).

60 Malkki, *Purity and Exile* (n. 58), 112.

61 Ibid., 137. She seems inspired by M. Foucault (2002) *The Order of Things: An Archaeology of the Human Sciences* (London: Routledge).

62 Turner, *Politics of Innocence* (n. 58), 8. On Schmitt's 'state of exception' see M. Luoma-Aho (2000) 'Carl Schmitt and the Transformation of the Political Subject', *European Legacy*, 5:5, 703–716.

63 Turner: *Politics of Innocence* (n. 58), 43–64. On Weber's theory of bureaucracy see H. Constas (1958) 'Max Weber's Two Conceptions of Bureaucracy', *American Journal of Sociology*, 563:4, 400–409; G. Ritzer (1975) 'Professionalization and Rationalization: The Views of Max Weber', *Social Forces*, 53:4, 627–634; J. O'Neill (1986) 'The Disciplinary Society: From Weber to Foucault', *British Journal of Sociology*, 37:1, 42–60. On biopolitics see M. Foucault (1998) *The History of Sexuality*, vol.1: *The Will to Knowledge* (Harmondsworth: Penguin), 135–159; idem (2004) *Society Must Be Defended: Lectures at the Collège de France, 1975–1976* (London: Penguin), 238–263, especially 243. See also J. Reid (2010) 'The Biopolitization and Humanitarianism: From Saving Bare Life to Securing the Biohuman in Post-Interventionary Societies', *Journal of Interventionism and Statebuilding*, 4:4, 391–411; M.G. Doucet and M. de Larrinaga (2011) 'Human Security and the Securing of Human Life: Tracing Global Sovereign and Biopolitical Rule', in D. Chandler and N. Hynek (eds.) *Critical Perspectives on Human Security: Rethinking Emancipation and Power in International Relations* (London: Routledge), 129–143.

64 Turner, *Politics of Innocence* (n. 58), 47–49.

DOI: 10.1057/9781137502797.0009

65   G. Agamben (1998) *Homo Sacer: Sovereign Power and Bare Life* (Stanford, CA: Stanford University Press), 78. See also A. Feldman (2010) 'Inhumanitas: Political Speciation, Animality, Natality, Defacement,' in I. Feldman and M. Ticktin (eds.) *In the Name of Humanity: The Government of Threat and Care* (Durham, NC: Duke University Press), 115–150.

66   C. Horst (2006) *Transnational Nomads: How Somalis Cope with Refugee Life in the Dadaab Camps of Kenya* (New York: Berghahn Books); A.M. Abdi (2005) 'In Limbo: Dependency, Insecurity, and Identity amongst Somali Refugees in Dadaab Camps,' *Refuge*, 22:2, 6–14; J. Crisp (2000) 'A State of Insecurity: The Political Economy of Violence in Kenya's Refugee Camps,' *African Affairs*, 99:397, 601–632; A. Aubone and J. Hernandez (2013) 'Assessing Refugee Camp Characteristics and the Occurrence of Sexual Violence: A Preliminary Analysis of the Dadaab Complex,' *Refugee Survey Quarterly*, 32:4, 22–40.

67   Horst, *Transnational Nomads* (n. 66), 11.

68   Ibid., 13.

69   Ibid., 91–106.

70   M. Agier (2011) *Managing the Undesirables: Refugee Camps and Humanitarian Government* (Cambridge: Polity Press), 155. See also idem (2010) 'Humanity as an Identity and Its Political Effects (A Note on Camps and Humanitarian Government),' *Humanity*, 1:1, 29–45; idem (2008) *On the Margins of the World: The Refugee Experience Today* (Cambridge: Polity Press).

71   Agier, *Managing the Undesirables* (n. 70), 72, 77 and 79.

72   Horst, *Transnational Nomads* (n. 66), 161–200, quote from 163.

73   D. Fassin (2012) 'Compassion Protocol: Legalizing Diseased Undocumented Immigrants,' in idem *Humanitarian Reason: A Moral History of the Present* (Berkeley, CA: University of California Press), 83–108; idem (2010) 'Inequality of Lives, Hierarchies of Humanity: Moral Commitments and Ethical Dilemmas of Humanitarianism,' in Feldman and Ticktin (eds.) *In the Name of Humanity* (n. 65), 238–255.

74   Idem (2012) 'Truth Ordeal: Attesting Violence for Asylum Seekers,' in idem *Humanitarian Reason* (n. 73), 109–129.

75   Idem (2012) 'Hierarchies of Humanity: Intervening in International Conflicts,' in idem *Humanitarian Reason* (n. 73), 223–242, especially 226. See also idem (2009) 'Another Politics of Life Is Possible,' *Theory, Culture and Society*, 26:5, 44–60; idem (2006) 'La biopolitique n'est pas une politique de la vie,' *Sociologie et sociétés*, 38:2, 35–48; idem (2007) 'Humanitarianism as a Politics of Life,' *Public Culture*, 19:3, 499–520.

76   F.C. Cuny (1977) 'Refugee Camps and Camp Planning: The State of the Art,' *Disasters*, 1:2, 125–143; A. Ramadan (2012) 'Spatialising the Refugee Camp,' *Transactions of the Institute of British Geographers*, 38:1, 65–77. See also Malkki, *Purity and Exile* (n. 58), 38–47; Turner, *Politics of Innocence* (n. 322), 14–19; Horst, *Transnational Nomads* (n. 66), 78–86.

DOI: 10.1057/9781137502797.0009

77   F. Terry (2002) *Condemned to Repeat? The Paradox of Humanitarian Action* (Ithaca, NY: Cornell University Press), 114–215.

78   B. Lukunka (2012) 'New Big Men: Refugee Emasculation as a Human Security Issue,' *International Migration*, 50:5, 130–141; R. Horn (2010) 'Exploring the Impact of Displacement and Encampment on Domestic Violence in Kakuma Refugee Camp,' *Journal of Refugee Studies*, 23:3, 356–376; O.E. Olsen and K. S. Scharffseher (2004) 'Rape in Refugee Camps as Organisational Failures,' *International Journal of Human Rights*, 8:4, 377–397.

79   On Sudanese refugees in Uganda see T. Kaiser (2007) '"Moving Up and Down Looking for Money": Making a Living in a Ugandan Refugee Camp,' in J. Staples (ed.) *Livelihoods at the Margins: Surviving the City* (Walnut Creek, CA: Left Coast Press), 215–236; E. Werker (2007) 'Refugee Camp Economics,' *Journal of Refugee Studies*, 20:3, 461–480.

80   On the concept see Commission on Human Security (2003) *Human Security Now* (New York: Commission on Human Security); R. Paris (2001) 'Human Security: Paradigm Shift or Hot Air?,' *International Security*, 26:2, 87–102; E. Newman (2001) 'Human Security and Constructivism,' *International Studies Perspectives*, 2:3, 239–251; S. McFarlane et al. (2006) *Human Security and the UN: A Critical History* (Bloomington, IN: Indiana University Press).

81   R. Whitaker (1998) 'Refugees: The Security Dimension,' *Citizenship Studies*, 2:3, 413–434.

82   E. Mogire (2011) *Victims as Security Threats: Refugee Impact on Host State Security in Africa* (Farham, Surrey: Ashgate).

83   O. Wæver (1995) 'Securitization and Desecuritization,' in R.D. Lipschutz (ed.) *On Security* (New York: Columbia University Press), 46–86; B. Buzan et al. (1998) *Security: A New Framework for Analysis* (Boulder, CO: Lynne Rienner), 21–47; B. Buzan and L. Hansen (2009) *The Evolution of International Security Studies* (Cambridge: Cambridge University Press), 212–221; T. Balzacq (2005) 'The Three Faces of Securitization: Political Agency, Audience and Context,' *European Journal of International Relations*, 11:2, 171–201; idem (2011) 'A Theory of Securitization: Origins, Assumptions, and Variants,' in idem (ed.) *Understanding Securitization Theory* (London: Routledge), 1–30.

84   M. Enghoff et al. (2010) *In Search of Protection and Livelihoods: Socio-economic and Environmental Impacts of Dadaab Refugee Camps on Host Communities* (Copenhagen: Danida).

85   Mogire, *Victims as Security Threats* (n. 82), 79–100.

86   M. Bøås and K. Dunn (2013) *Politics of Origin in Africa: Autochthony, Citizenship and Conflict* (London: Zed); J-F. Bayart et al. (2001) 'Autochtonie, démocratie et citoyenneté en Afrique,' *Critique Internationale*, 10, 177–194.

87   A.K. Onoma (2013) *Anti-Refugee Violence and African Politics* (Cambridge: Cambridge University Press).

DOI: 10.1057/9781137502797.0009

88   S. Stedman and F. Tanner, eds. (2003) *Refugee Manipulation: War, Politics, and the Abuse of Human Suffering* (Washington, DC: Brookings Institution); Mogire, *Victims as Security Threats* (n. 82), 29–48; R. Muggah, ed. (2006) *No Refuge: The Crisis of Refugee Militarization in Africa* (London: Zed Books); K. Harpviken et al. (2013) 'Refugee Militancy in Exile and Upon Return in Afghanistan and Rwanda,' in J.T. Checkel (ed.) *Transnational Dynamics of Civil War* (Cambridge: Cambridge University Press), 89–119.

89   A. Zelberg et al. (1989) *Escape from Violence: Conflict and the Refugee Crisis in the Developing World* (Oxford: Oxford University Press), 275–278; H. Adelman (1998) 'Why Refugee Warriors Are Threats,' *Journal of Conflict Studies*, 18:1, 49–69; K. Newland (1993) 'Ethnic Conflict and Refugees,' *Survival*, 35:1, 81–101.

90   I. Salehyan (2007) 'Transnational Rebels: Neighbouring States as Sanctuary for Rebel Groups,' *World Politics*, 59:2, 217–242; idem and K.S. Gleditsch (2006) 'Refugees and the Spread of Civil War,' *International Organization*, 60:2, 335–366; A. Dowty and G. Loescher (1996) 'Refugee Flows as Grounds for International Action,' *International Security*, 21:1, 43–71.

91   S.L. Carruthers (2005) 'Between Caps: Eastern Bloc "Escapees" and Cold War Borderlands,' *American Quarterly*, 57:3, 911–942; J.J. Carafano (1999) 'Mobilizing Europe's Stateless: America's Plans for a Cold War Army,' *Journal of Cold War Studies*, 1:2, 61–85; C. Tudda (2005) '"Reenacting the Story of Tantalus": Eisenhower, Dulles, and the Failed Rhetoric of Liberation,' ibid., 7:4, 3–35; G. Bischof (2006) 'The Collapse of Liberation Rhetoric: The Eisenhower Administration and the 1956 Hungarian Crisis,' *Hungarian Studies*, 20:1, 51–63.

92   J. Ranelagh (1987) *The Agency: The Rise and Decline of the CIA*. 2nd ed. (New York: Simon and Schuster), 349–382; Z. Karabell (1999) *Architects of Intervention: The United States, the Third World, and the Cold War 1946–1962* (Baton Rouge, LA: Louisiana State University Press), 173–205; P. Gleijeses (1995) 'Ships in the Night: The CIA, the White House and the Bay of Pigs,' *Journal of Latin American Studies*, 27:1, 1–42; M. Smith (2004) 'The United States' Use of Exiles in Promoting Regime Change in Cuba, 1961 and Iraq, 2002–3,' *Small Wars and Insurgencies*, 15:1, 38–53.

93   P.W. Rodman (1994) *More Precious than Peace: The Cold War and the Struggle for the Third World* (New York: Charles Scribner's Sons), 222–256; J.M. Scott (1996) *Deciding to Intervene: The Reagan Doctrine and American Foreign Policy* (Durham, NC: Duke University Press), 152–192; G. Loescher (1988) 'Humanitarianism and Politics in Central America,' *Political Science Quarterly*, 103:2, 295–320; P.L. Shepherd (1984) 'The Tragic Course and Consequences of U.S. Policy in Honduras,' *World Policy Journal*, 2:1, 109–154; S. Macekura (2011) '"For Fear of Persecution": Displaced Salvadorans and U.S. Refugee

DOI: 10.1057/9781137502797.0009

Policy in the 1980s,' *Journal of Policy History*, 23:3, 357–380; Terry, *Condemned to Repeat?* (n. 77), 83–113.

94 Sayigh, *Armed Struggle and the Search for State* (n. 54), 262–268; A. Abu-Odeh (1999) *Jordanians, Palestinians and the Hashemite Kingdom in the Middle East Peace Process* (Washington, DC: United States Institute for Peace Press), 169–192; M.S. Braizat (1998) *The Jordanian Palestinian Relationship: The Bankruptcy of the Confederal Idea* (London: British Academic Press), 137–142; S. Al-Khazendar (1997) *Jordan and the Palestine Question: The Role of Islamic and Left Forces in Foreign Policy-Making* (Reading: Ithaca Press).

95 F. El Khazen (2000) *The Breakdown of the State in Lebanon, 1967–1976* (London: I.B. Tauris), 129–202, 361–378; Sayigh, *Armed Struggle and the Search for State* (n. 54), 188–194, 373–409.

96 A. Plascov (1981) *The Palestinian Refugees in Jordan 1948–1957* (London: Frank Cass), 92–103; M.C. Hudson (1972) 'Developments and Setbacks in the Palestinian Resistance Movement 1967–1971,' *Journal of Palestine Studies*, 1:3, 64–84.

97 R. Leenders (2009) 'Refugee Warriors or War Refugees? Iraqi Refugees' Predicament in Syria, Jordan and Lebanon,' *Mediterranean Politics*, 14:3, 343–363; idem (2008) 'Iraqi Refugees in Syria: Causing a Spill-over of the Iraqi Conflict?' *Third World Quarterly*, 29:8, 1563–1584; International Crisis Group, ICG (2008) 'Failed Responsibility: Iraqi Refugees in Syria, Jordan and Lebanon,' *Middle East Report*, 77 (Brussels: ICG); S.K. Lischer (2008) 'Security and Displacement in Iraq: Responding to the Forced Displacement Crisis,' *International Security*, 33:2, 95–119; A. Harper (2008) 'Iraq's Refugees: Ignored and Unwanted,' *International Review of the Red Cross*, 90:869, 169–190.

98 K. McConnachie (2012) 'Rethinking the "Refugee Warrior": The Karen National Union and Refugee Protection on the Thai-Burma Border,' *Journal of Human Rights Practice*, 4:1, 30–56.

99 C. Robinson (2000) 'Refugee Warriors at the Thai-Cambodian Border,' *Refugee Survey Quarterly*, 19:1, 23–37; Terry, *Condemned to Repeat?* (n. 77), 114–154.

100 D. Unger (2003) 'Ain't Enough Blanket: International Humanitarian Assistance and Cambodian Political Resistance,' in Stedman and Tanner (eds.) *Refugee Manipulation* (n.352), 17–56; Kiernan, *The Pol Pot Regime* (n. 256), 440–465; T. Findlay (1996) 'Turning the Corner in Southeast Asia,' in M.E. Brown (ed.) *The International Dimensions of Internal Conflict* (Cambridge, MA: MIT Press), 173–204, especially 197–199; S.J. Morris (1999) *Why Vietnam Invaded Cambodia: Political Culture and the Causes of the War* (Stanford, CA: Stanford University Press), 97–102.

101 S.K. Lischer (2005) *Dangerous Sanctuaries: Refugee Camps, Civil War, and the Dilemmas of Humanitarian Aid* (Ithaca, NY: Cornell University Press),

DOI: 10.1057/9781137502797.0009

44–72; Terry, *Condemned to Repeat?* (n. 77), 55–82; F. Grare (2003) 'The Geopolitics of Afghan Refugees in Pakistan,' in Stedman and Tanner (eds.) *Refugee Manipulation* (n. 88), 57–94; N. Nojumi (2002) *The Rise of the Taliban in Afghanistan: Mass Mobilization, Civil War, and the Future of the Region* (Houndmills: Palgrave Macmillan), 122–124; R.D. Kaplan (2001) *Soldiers of God: With Islamic Warriors in Afghanistan and Pakistan* (New York: Vintage); A. Rashid (2001) *Taliban: Militant Islam, Oil and Fundamentalism in Central Asia* (New Haven, CT: Yale University Press); B.G. Williams (2008) 'Talibanistan: History of a Transnational Terrorist Sanctuary,' *Civil Wars*, 10:1, 40–59; M. Urban (1988) *War in Afghanistan* (New York: St. Martin's Press), 77–78. On the Pakistani madrassahs C. Fair (2008) *The Madrassah Challenge: Militancy and Religious Education in Pakistan* (Washington, DC: United States Institute for Peace Press); International Crisis Group (2005) 'Pakistan: Madrasas, Extremism and the Military,' *ICG Asia Report*, 36 (Brussels: ICG).

102 J. Young (1998) 'The Tigray People's Liberation Front,' in C. Clapham (ed.) *African Guerrillas* (Oxford: James Currey), 36–52, especially 44–46; B. Hendrie (1994) 'Relief Aid behind the Lines: The Cross-Border Operation in Tigray,' in J. Macrae and A. Zwi (eds.) *War and Hunger: Rethinking International Responses to Complex Emergencies* (London: Zed), 125–138.

103 D. Pool (1998) 'The Eritrean People's Liberation Front,' in Clapham (ed.) *African Guerrillas* (n. 102), 19–35; idem (2001) *From Guerrillas to Government: The Eritrean People's Liberation Front* (Oxford: James Currey), 129–131; L. Cliffe (1994) 'The Impact of War on Food Security in Eritrea: Prospects for Recovery,' in Macrae and Zwi (eds.) *War and Hunger* (n. 102), 160–178; G. Kibreab (2009) *Eritrea: A Dream Referred* (Suffolk: James Currey), 67–70.

104 Mogire, *Victims as Security Threats* (n. 82), 121–123. On OLF see A. De Waal (1997) *Famine Crimes: Politics and the Disaster Relief Industry in Africa* (Oxford: James Currey), 148–150; D. Keen (2008) *The Benefits of Famine: A Political Economy of Famine and Relief in Southwestern Sudan 1983–89.* 2nd ed. (Oxford: James Currey), 144–147, 177, 201–210.

105 Lischer, *Dangerous Sanctuaries* (n. 101), 1–43.

106 For a contrary view see E. Mogire (2006) 'Preventing or Abetting: Refugee Militarization in Tanzania,' in Muggah (ed.) *No Refuge* (n. 352), 137–178.

107 Lischer, *Dangerous Sanctuaries* (n. 101), 6.

108 Ibid., 21; K. Koser (1997) 'Information and Repatriation: The Case of Mozambican Refugees in Malawi,' *Journal of Refugee Studies*, 10:1, 1–17; R.T. Huffman (1992) 'Repatriation of Refugees from Malawi to Mozambique,' *Africa Today*, 39:1–2 , 114–122. On the civil war and Renamo see M. Hall (1990) 'The Mozambican National Resistance Movement (RENAMO): A Study in the Destruction of an African Country,' *Africa*, 60:1, 39–68; G. Morgan (1990) 'Violence in Mozambique: Towards an Understanding of

DOI: 10.1057/9781137502797.0009

Renamo,' *Journal of Modern African Studies*, 28:4, 603–619; T. Young (1990)
'The MNR/RENAMO: External and Internal Dynamics,' *African Affairs*,
89:357, 491–509; K.B. Wilson (1992) 'Cults of Violence and Counterviolence
in Mozambique,' *Journal of Southern African Studies*, 18:3, 527–582; L. Hultman
(2009) 'The Power to Hurt in Civil War: The Strategic Aim of RENAMO
Violence,' ibid., 35:4, 821–834. On the 'Rhodesian' and South African
sponsorship see W. Minter (1994) *Apartheid's Contras: An Inquiry into the
Roots of War in Angola and Mozambique* (London: Zed Books); T. Ohlson
et al. (1994) *The New Is Not Yet Born: Conflict Resolution in Southern Africa*
(Washington, DC: Brookings Institution), 64–75.

109 N.M. Birkeland and A.U. Gomes (2000) 'Angola: *Deslocados* in the Province
of Huambo,' *Norwegian Journal of Geography*, 54:3, 17–47; T. Hodges (2001)
Angola from Afro-Stalinism to Petro-Diamond Capitalism (Oxford: James
Currey), 21–23, 31–32; D. Hilhorst and M. Serrano (2010) 'The Humanitarian
Arena in Angola, 1975–2008,' *Disasters*, 34:S2, 183–201.

110 G.R. Berridge (1990) 'The Superpowers and Southern Africa,' in R. Allison
and P. Williams (eds.) *Superpower Competition and Crisis Prevention in the
Third World* (Cambridge: Cambridge University Press), 206–226. On the
US involvement, see J.E. Davies (2007) *Constructive Engagement? Chester
Crocker and American Policy in South Africa, Namibia and Angola* (Oxford:
James Currey), written as a response to C. Crocker (1992) *High Noon in
Southern Africa: Making Peace in a Rough Neighborhood* (New York: Norton).
On the Soviet role see V. Shubin (2008) *The Hot 'Cold War.' The USSR in
Southern Africa* (London: Pluto Press). On Cuba's involvement see E. George
(2005) *The Cuban Intervention in Angola, 1965–1991: From Che Guevara to
Cuito Cuanavale* (London: Frank Cass). On China see S.F. Jackson (1995)
'China's Third World Foreign Policy: The Case of Angola and Mozambique,
1961–93,' *China Quarterly*, 142, 388–422; and on South Africa's role see Minter,
Apartheid's Contras (n. 108); O. Ibeanu (1990) 'Apartheid, Destabilization
and Displacement: The Dynamics of the Refugee Crises in Southern Africa,'
Journal of Refugee Studies, 3:1, 47–63.

111 On Mozambique see C. Hume (1994) *Ending Mozambique's War: The Role
of Mediation and Good Offices* (Washington, DC: USIP); R. Synge (1997)
Mozambique: UN Peacekeeping in Action, 1992–94 (Washington, DC: USIP); A.
Ajello (1999) 'Mozambique: Implementation of the 1992 Peace Agreement,'
in C.A. Crocker et. al. (eds.) *Herding Cats: Multiparty Mediation in a Complex
World* (Washington, DC: USIP), 615–642; S. Barnes (1998) 'Peacekeeping
in Mozambique,' in O. Furley and R. May (eds.) *Peacekeeping in Africa*
(Aldershot: Ashgate), 159–178. On Angola see P. Hare (1998) *Angola's Last
Best Chance for Peace: An Insider's Account of the Peace Process* (Washington,
DC: USIP); M.J. Anstee (1998) 'The United Nations in Angola: Post-
Bicesse Implementation,' in Crocker et al. (eds.) *Herding Cats*, 589–613; D.

DOI: 10.1057/9781137502797.0009

Rothchild and C. Hartzell (1995) 'Interstate and Intrastate Negotiations in Angola', in I.W. Zartman (ed.) *Elusive Peace: Negotiating an End to Civil Wars* (Washington, DC: Brookings Institution), 175–203.

112   H. Adelman (2003) 'The Use and Abuse of Refugees in Zaïre', in Stedman and Tanner (eds.) *Refugee Manipulation* (n.88), 95–134; C. Lepora and R.E. Goodin (2011) 'Grading Complicity in Rwandan Refugee Camps', *Journal of Applied Philosophy*, 28:3, 259–276; Terry, *Condemned to Repeat?* (n. 77), 155–215.

113   M.L. Christian (1998) 'A Lesson Unlearned: The Unjust Revolution in Rwanda, 1959–1961', *Emory International Law Review*, 12:3, 1271–1329; K. Long (2012) 'Rwanda's First Refugees: Tutsi Exile and International Response 1959–64', *Journal of Eastern African Studies*, 6:2, 211–229; R. van der Meeren (1996) 'Three Decades in Exile: Rwandan Refugees 1960–1990', *Journal of Refugee Studies*, 9:3, 252–267.

114   P. Reyntjens (1996) 'Rwanda: Genocide and Beyond', *Journal of Refugee Studies*, 9:3, 240–251, especially 246.

115   On the RPF/A see G. Prunier (1998) 'The Rwandan Patriotic Front', in Clapham (ed.) *African Guerrillas* (n. 102), 119–133; W.C. Reed (1996) 'Exile, Reform, and the Rise of the Rwandan Patriotic Front', *Journal of Modern African Studies*, 34:3, 479–501. On the NRA see M. Mamdani (1988) 'Uganda in Transition: Two Years of the NRA/NRM', *Third World Quarterly*, 10:3, 1155–1181; N. Kasfir (2005) 'Dilemmas of Popular Support in Guerrilla War: The National Resistance Army in Uganda, 1981–86', *Journal of Modern African Studies*, 43:2, 271–296; P. Ngoga (1998) 'Uganda: The National Resistance Army', in Clapham (ed.) *African Guerrillas* (n. 102), 91–106; E. Katumba-Wamala (2000) 'The National Resistance Army (NRA) as a Guerrilla Force', *Small Wars and Insurgencies*, 11:3, 160–171; J.M. Weinstein (2007) *Inside Rebellion: The Politics of Insurgent Violence* (Cambridge: Cambridge University Press), 62–71, 108–111, 140–145, 175–180, 219–229, 265–270.

116   O. Ottunu (2000) 'A Historical Analysis of the Invasion by the Rwanda Patriotic Army (RPA)', in H. Adelman and A. Suhrke (eds.) *The Path of a Genocide: The Rwanda Crisis from Uganda to Zaire* (New Brunswick, NJ: Transaction Publishers), 31–49.

117   M. Mamdani (2011) *When Victims Become Killers: Colonialism, Nativism, and the Genocide in Rwanda* (Oxford: James Currey), 210–214; G. Prunier (1999) *The Rwanda Crisis: History of a Genocide.* 2nd ed. (Kampala: Fountain Publishers), 159–197; L. Melvern (2000) *A People Betrayed: The Role of the West in Rwanda's Genocide* (London: Zed Books), 52–60; idem (2004) *Conspiracy to Murder: The Rwandan Genocide* (London: Verso), 59–64; B.D. Jones (2000) 'The Arusha Peace Process', in Adelman and Suhrke, *The Path of a Genocide* (n. 116), 131–156; M. Barnett (2003) *Eyewitness to a Genocide:*

DOI: 10.1057/9781137502797.0009

The United Nations and Rwanda (Ithaca, NY: Cornell University Press), 49–96.

118 On the genocide as such see the following books: A. De Forges (1999) *Leave None to Tell the Story: Genocide in Rwanda* (New York: Human Rights Watch); Prunier, *The Rwanda Crisis* (n. 117); Mamdani, *When Victims become Killers* (n. 117); S.M. Khan (2000) *The Shallow Graves of Rwanda* (London: I.B. Tauris); R. Dallaire (2003) *Shake Hands with the Devil: The Failure of Humanity in Rwanda* (Toronto: Random House Canada); J.A. Berry and C.P. Berry, eds. (1999) *Genocide in Rwanda: A Collective Memory* (Washington, DC: Howard University Press); S. Straus (2006) *The Order of Genocide: Race, Power and War in Rwanda* (Ithaca, NY: Cornell University Press); N. Eltringham (2004) *Accounting for Horror: Genocide Debates in Rwanda* (London: Pluto Press); Melvern, *A People Betrayed* (n. 117); idem, *Conspiracy to Murder* (n. 117); P. Gourevitch (2000) *We Wish to Inform You that Tomorrow We Will be Killed with Our Families: Stories from Rwanda* (London: Picador).

119 B. Rutinwa (1996) 'The Tanzanian Government's Response to the Rwandan Emergency', *Journal of Refugee Studies*, 9:3, 291–302.

120 C. Fisiy (1998) 'Of Journeys and Border Crossings: Return of Refugees, Identity, and Reconstruction in Rwanda', *African Studies Review*, 41:1, 17–28; S.K. Lischer (2011) 'Civil War, Genocide and Political Order in Rwanda: Security Implications of Refugee Return', *Conflict, Security and Development*, 11:3, 261–284; K. Halvorsen (2000) 'Protection and Humanitarian Assistance in the Refugee Camps in Zaïre: The Problem of Security', in Adelman and Suhrke, *The Path of a Genocide* (n. 116), 307–320.

121 On the widespread involvement of civilians in the Rwandan genocide see S. Straus (2004) 'How Many Perpetrators Were There in the Rwandan Genocide?' *Journal of Genocide Research*, 6:1, 85–98.

122 G. Prunier (2000) 'Opération Turquoise: A Humanitarian Escape from a Political Dead End', in Adelman and Suhrke, *The Path of a Genocide* (n. 116), 281–305; idem, *The Rwanda Crisis* (n. 117), 281–311; A. Wallis (2006) *Silent Accomplice: The Untold Story of France's Role in the Rwandan Genocide* (London: I.B. Tauris), 122–145; D. Kroslak (2007) *The Role of France in the Rwandan Genocide* (London: Hurst), 212–219, 227–241; Dallaire, *Shake Hands with the Devil* (n. 117), 431–458; Melvern, *A People Betrayed* (n. 116), 210–226.

123 A. Storey (1997) 'Non-Neutral Humanitarianism: NGOs and the Rwanda Crisis', *Development in Practice*, 7:4, 384–394; J. Pottier (1996) 'Relief and Repatriation: Views by Rwandan Refugees; Lessons for the Humanitarian Aid Workers', *African Affairs*, 95:380, 403–429; B. Barber (1997) 'Feeding Refugees, or War? The Dilemma of Humanitarian Aid', *Foreign Affairs*, 76:4, 8–14; F. Fox (2001) 'New Humanitarianism: Does It Provide a Moral Banner for the 21st Century', *Disasters*, 25:4, 275–289; J. Boutroue (1998) 'Missed Opportunities: The Role of the International Community in the

DOI: 10.1057/9781137502797.0009

Return of the Rwandan Refugees from Eastern Zaïre July 1994–December 1996,' *Rosemay Rogers Working Paper Series*, 1 (Inter-University Committee on International Migration), at http://web.mit.edu/cis/www/migration/pubs/rrwp/1_missedop.pdf; K. Mills (2004) 'Refugee Return from Zaire to Rwanda: The Role of the UNHCR,' in H. Adelman and G.C. Rao (eds.) *War and Peace in Zaire/Congo* (Trenton, NJ: Africa World Press), 163–185; F. Terry (2004) 'The Humanitarian Impulse: Imperatives versus Consequences,' ibid., 187–251; idem, *Condemned to Repeat?* (n. 341), 125–215.

124　The most elaborate analysis of the humanitarian assistance is vol. 3 on 'Humanitarian Aid and Effects' of the 5-volume *Joint Evaluation of Emergency Assistance to Rwanda* (Copenhagen: Steering Committee of the Joint Evaluation of Emergency Assistance to Rwanda, 1996), compiled by a core team led by J. Borton. The gist of the assessment is also published in idem (1996) 'An Account of Co-ordination Mechanisms for Humanitarian Assistance in Rwanda,' *Disasters*, 20:4, 305–323. On its impact see idem and J. Erikson (2004) *Lessons from Rwanda: Lessons for Today. Assessment of the Impact and Influence of the Joint Evaluation of Emergency Assistance to Rwanda* (www.alnap.org/resource/3354). See also A. Storey (1997) 'Non-Neutral Humanitarianism: NGOs and the Rwanda Crisis,' *Development in Practice*, 7:4, 384–394; I. Martin (1998) 'Hard Choices after Genocide: Human Rights and Political Failures in Rwanda,' in J. Moore (ed.) *Hard Choices: Moral Dilemmas in Humanitarian Intervention* (Lanham, MD: Rowman and Littlefield), 157–175; S.K. Lischer (2003) 'Collateral Damage: Humanitarian Assistance as a Cause of Conflict,' *International Security*, 28:1, 79–109.

125　A. Cooley and J. Ron (2002) 'The NGO Scramble: Organizational Insecurity and the Political Economy of Transnational Action,' *International Security*, 27:1, 5–39; See also T.G. Weiss (2013) *Humanitarian Business* (Hoboken, NJ: Wiley); J. Goodhand (2006) *Aiding Peace? The Role of NGOs in Armed Conflict* (Boulder, CO: Lynne Rienner); D. Rieff (2002) *A Bed for the Night: Humanitarianism in Crisis* (London: Vintage), 155–193.

126　J.C. Hammock and J.R. Charny (1996) 'Emergency Response as Morality Play: The Media, the Relief Agencies, and the Need for Capacity Building,' in R.I. Rotberg and T. Weiss (eds.) *From Massacres to Genocide: The Media, Public Policy, and Humanitarian Crisis* (Washington, DC: Brookings Institution), 115–135; L. Hilsum (2007) 'Reporting Rwanda: The Media and the Aid Agencies,' in A. Thompson (ed.) *The Media and the Rwandan Genocide* (London: Pluto Press), 167–187; R. Dowden (2004) 'Comment: The Rwandan Genocide: How the Press Missed the Story,' *African Affairs*, 103:411, 283–290.

127　All documents are available at the website of the Steering Committee at http://schr.info/resources and http://schr.info/certification. See also L. Gostelow (1999) 'The Sphere Project: The Implications of Making

Humanitarian Principles and Codes Work,' *Disasters*, 23:4, 316–325; P. Walker and S. Purdin (2004) 'Birthing Sphere,' ibid., 28:2, 100–111; D. Hilhorst (2005) 'Dead Letter or Living Document? Ten Years of the Code of Conduct for Disaster Relief,' ibid., 29:4, 351–369; P. Walker et al. (2010) 'A Blueprint for Professionalizing Humanitarian Assistance,' *Health Affairs*, 29:12, 2223–2230.

128 K. Mills and R. Norton (2002) 'Refugees and Security in the Great Lakes of Africa,' *Civil Wars*, 5:1, 1–26; B.E. Whitaker (2003) 'Refugees and the Spread of Conflict: Contrasting Cases in Central Africa,' *Journal of Asian and African Studies*, 38:2–3, 211–231.

129 M. Rafti (2006) 'Rwanda Hutu Rebels in Congo-Zaïre, 1994–2006: An Extra-Territorial Civil War in a Weak State,' *L'Afrique des Grands Lacs. Annuaire 2005–2006* (Paris: L'Harmattan), 55–83; A. Gnamo (2000) 'The Rwandan Genocide and the Collapse of Mobutu's Kleptocracy,' in Adelman and Suhrke, *The Path of a Genocide* (n. 116), 321–349, especially 327–330; idem (2004) 'The Role of the Interahamwe in the Regional Conflict: The Origins of Unrest in Kivu, Zaire,' in Adelman and Rao (eds.) *War and Peace* (n. 123), 85–107; K. Vlassenroot (2006) 'A Societal View on Violence and War: Conflict and Militia Formation in Eastern Congo,' in P. Kaarsholm (ed.) *Violence, Political Culture and Development in Africa* (Oxford: James Currey), 49–65; International Crisis Group (2005) 'The Congo: Solving the FDLR Problem Once and for All,' *Africa Briefing*: 25 (Brussels: ICG).

130 F. Van Acker and K. Vlassenroot (2001) 'Les 'mai-mai' et les fonctions de la violence milicienne dans l'est du Congo,' *Politique Africaine*, 84, 103–116; A.M. Bwenge (2003), 'Les milices Mayi-mayi à l'est de la République du Congo,' *Revue Africaine de Sociologie*, 7:2, 73–94.

131 T. Turner (2007) *The Congo War: Conflict, Myth, Reality* (London: Zed Books), 76–105; F. Reyntjens (2009) *The Great African War: Congo and the Regional Geopolitics, 1996–2006* (Cambridge: Cambridge University Press), 21–23; G. Prunier (2009) *From Genocide to Continental War: The 'Congolese' Conflict and the Crisis of Contemporary Africa* (London: Hurst), 51–53; J.K. Stearns (2011) *Dancing in the Glory of Monsters: The Collapse of the Congo and the Great War of Africa* (New York: Public Affairs), 57–67.

132 W.C. Reed (1998): 'Guerrillas in the Midst: The Former Government of Rwanda (FGOR) and the Alliance of Democratic Forces for the Liberation of Congo-Zaïre (ADFL) in Eastern Zaïre,' in Clapham (ed.) *African Guerrillas* (n. 102), 134–154; K.C. Dunn (2002) 'A Survival Guide to Kinshasa: Lessons of the Father, Passed Down to the Son,' in J.F. Clark (ed.) *The African Stakes of the Congo War* (New York: Palgrave Macmillan), 53–74; J-C. Willame (1999) *L'oddyssée Kabila: Trajectoire pour une Congo nouveau?* (Paris: Karthala), 15–50; D. Renton et al. (2007) *The Congo: Plunder and Resistance*

DOI: 10.1057/9781137502797.0009

(London: Zed Books), 184–188; Stearns, *Dancing in the Glory of Monsters* (n. 131), 81–90.

133 K.N.F. Emizet (2000) 'The Massacres of Refugees in Congo: A Case of UN Peacekeeping Failure and International Law', *Journal of Modern African Studies*, 38:2, 163–202.

134 O. Ottunnu (2004) 'Uganda as a Regional Actor in the Zairian War', in Adelman and Rao (eds.) *War and Peace* (n. 123), 31–83; J.F. Clark (2002) 'Museveni's Adventure in the Congo War: Uganda's Vietnam?' in idem (ed.) *The African Stakes of the Congo War* (n. 132), 145–165; T. Turner (2002) 'Angola's Role in the Congo War', ibid., 75–92; M.R. Rupiya (2002) 'A Political and Military Review of Zimbabwe's Involvement in the Second Congo War', ibid., 93–105; M. Nest (2001) 'Ambitions, Profits and Loss: Zimbabwean Economic Involvement in the Democratic Republic of the Congo', *African Affairs*, 100:400, 469–490; International Crisis Group (1999) 'Scramble for the Congo. Anatomy of an Ugly War', *ICG Africa Report*, 26 (Brussels: ICG); D. Shearer (1999) 'Africa's Great War', *Survival*, 41:2, 89–106.

135 M. Nest et al. (2006) *The Democratic Republic of Congo: Economic Dimensions of War and Peace* (Boulder, CO: Lynne Rienner); Renton et al., *The Congo* (n. 132); C. Braeckman (2003) *Les nouveaux prédateurs. Politique des poussances en Afrique centrale* (Paris: Fayard), 149–272.

136 International Rescue Committee (2003) *Mortality in the Democratic Republic of Congo: Results from a Nationwise Survey* (New York: IRC); B. Caghlan et al. (2006) 'Mortality in the Democratic Republic of Congo: A Nationwise Survey', *Lancet*, 367, 44–51; IRC (2007) *Measuring Mortality in the Democratic Republic of Congo* (New York: IRC).

137 Lischer, *Dangerous Sanctuaries* (n. 101), 11–12.

138 On the militarisation of the camps in Guinea see J. Millner (2005) 'The Militarization and Demilitarization of Refugee Camps in Guinea', in N. Florquin and E.G. Berman (eds.) *Armed and Aimless: Armed Groups, Guns, and Human Security in the ECOWAS Region* (Geneva: Small Arms Survey), 145–179; idem and A. Christoffersen-Deb (2006) 'The Militarization and Demilitarization of Refugee Camps and Settlements in Guinea, 1999–2004', in Muggah (ed.) *No Refuge* (n. 88), 51–89, especially 51–52. On LURD see W. Reno (2007) 'Liberia: The LURDs of the New Church', in M. Bøås and K.S. Dunn (eds.) *African Guerrillas: Raging against the Machine* (Boulder, CO: Lynne Rienner), 69–80; International Crisis Group (2002) 'Liberia: The Key to Ending Regional Instability', *Africa Report*, 43 (Brussels: ICG); Human Rights Watch (2001) 'Guinea. Refugees Still at Risk: Continuing Refugee Protection Concerns in Guinea', *HRW Report*, 13:5A; idem (2002) 'Guinea. Liberian Refugees in Guinea. Refoulement, Militarization of Camps, and Other Protection Concerns', ibid., 14:8A. On the background to the refugee flow see W. Van Damme (1999) 'How Liberian and Sierra Leonean Refugees

DOI: 10.1057/9781137502797.0009

Settled in the Forest Region of Guinea (1990–96); *Journal of Refugee Studies*, 12:1, 36–53.

139 Z. Al-Shaik (1984) 'Sabra and Shatila 1982: Resisting the Massacre; *Journal of Palestine Studies*, 14:1, 57–90; L. Shahid (2002) 'The Sabra and Shatila Massacres: Eye-Witness Reports; ibid., 32:1, 36–58; E. Siegel (2001) 'After Nineteen Years: Sabra and Shatila Remembered; *Middle East Policy*, 8:4, 86–100. On Sharon's responsibility see L.A. Malone (1985) 'The Kahan Report, Ariel Sharon and the Sabra-Shatila Massacres in Lebanon: Responsibility under International Law for Massacres of Civilian Populations; *Utah International Law Review*, 2, 373–434; Y. Shany and K.R. Michaeli (2002) 'The Case against Ariel Sharon: Revisiting the Doctrine of Command Responsibility; *New York Journal of International Law and Politics*, 34:4, 797–886.

140 See S. Allen (2010) 'Harboring or Protecting? Militarized Refugees, State Responsibility, and the Evolution of Self-Defense; *Praxis: The Fletcher Journal of Human Security*, 25:1, 5–22; M. Othman-Chande (1990) 'International Law and Armed Attacks in Refugee Camps; *Nordic Journal of International Law*, 2–3, 153–177.

141 S. Conway-Lanz (2005) 'Beyond No Gun Ri: Refugees and the United States Military in the Korean War; *Diplomatic History*, 29:1, 49–81; S. Choi (2008) 'Silencing Survivors' Narratives: Why Are We Forgetting the No Gun Ri Story?' *Rhetorics and Public Affairs*, 11:3, 367–388; T-U. Baik (2001) 'A War Crime Against an Ally's Civilians: The No Gun Ri Massacre; *Notre Dame Journal of Law, Ethics and Public Affairs*, 15:2, 455–505; C.J. Hanley (2010) 'No Gun Ri: Official Narrative and Inconvenient Truths; *Critical Asian Studies*, 42:4, 589–622.

142 M. Pugh (2004) 'Drowning Not Waving: Boat People and Humanitarianism at Sea; *Journal of Refugee Studies*, 17:1, 50–69; J.Z. Pugash (1977) 'The Dilemma of the Sea Refugee: Rescue Without Refuge; *Harvard International Law Journal*, 18:3, 577–604; R.P. Schaffer (1983) 'The Singular Plight of Sea-Borne Refugees; *Australian Yearbook of International Law*, 8, 213–234.

143 W.C. Robinson (1998) *Terms of Refuge: The Indochinese Exodus and the International Response* (London: Zed Books); S.E. Davies (2008) 'Realistic yet Humanitarian? The Comprehensive Plan of Action and Refugee Policy in Southeast Asia; *International Relations of the Asia-Pacific*, 8, 191–207.

144 S. Eklöf (2006) *Pirates in Paradise: A Modern History of Southeast Asia's Maritime Marauders* (Copenhagen: NIAS Press), 17–34, especially 26; Robinson, *Terms of Refuge* (no. 143), 166–171; V. Muntarbhorn (1981) 'Asylum-Seekers at Sea and Piracy in the Gulf of Thailand; *Revue beige de droit international*, 16, 483–508.

145 J.J.F. Espenilla (2010) 'Injustice Ignored: A Case Study of the Irregular Sea Migration of the Rohingyan Boat People; *Asia-Europe Journal*, 8:1, 45–59; C. Lewa (2008) 'Asia's New Boat People; *Forced Migration Review*, 30, 40–41;

DOI: 10.1057/9781137502797.0009

Human Rights Watch (2009) *Perilous Plight: Burma's Rohingya Take to the Seas* (New York: HRW).

146 A. Schloenhardt (2000) 'Australia and the Boat People: 25 Years of Unauthorized Arrivals,' *University of New South Wales Law Journal*, 23:3, 33–55.

147 A. Netherty et al. (2012) 'Exporting Detention: Australia-Funded Immigration Detention in Indonesia,' *Journal of Refugee Studies*, 26:1, 88–109; S. Taylor and B. Rafferty-Brown (2010) 'Waiting for Life to Begin: The Plight of Asylum Seekers Caught by Australia's Indonesian Solution,' *International Journal of Refugee Law*, 22:4, 558–592.

148 P.D. Fox (2013) 'International Asylum and Boat People: The Tampa Affair and Australia's "Pacific Solution",' *Maryland Journal of International Law*, 25:1, 356–373; J.E. Tauman (2002) 'Comment: Rescued at Sea, but Nowhere to Go: The Cloudy Legal Waters of the Tampa Crisis,' *Pacific Rim Law and Policy Journal*, 11:2, 461–492; M. Crock (2003) 'In the Wake of the *Tampa*: Conflicting Visions of International Refugee Law in the Management of Refugee Flows,' ibid., 12:1, 49–95; P. Matthew (2002) 'Australian Refugee Protection in the Wake of the Tampa,' *American Journal of International Law*, 96:3, 661–676.

149 The international conventions include the Safety of Life Convention (SOLAS) of 1974, the UN Convention of the Law of the Sea (UNCLOS) of 1982 and the International Convention on Maritime Search and Rescue (SAR) of 1979. They are all available at the website of the International Maritime Organization (IMO) at www.imo.org/About/Conventions/ListOfConventions/Pages/Default.aspx.

150 F. McKay et al. (2011) '"Any One of These Boat People Could Be a Terrorist for All We Know!" Media Representations and Public Perceptions of "Boat People" Arrivals in Australia,' *Journalism*, 12:5, 607–626; J. McAdam and K. Purcell (2008) 'Refugee Protection in the Howard Years: Obstructing the Right to Asylum,' *Australian Yearbook of International Law*, 27, 87–113.

151 E.A. Stratton (1986) *Plymouth Colony, Its History and People, 1620–1691* (USA: Ancestry Publishing), 17–37; M.L. Sargent (1988) 'The Conservative Covenant: The Rise of the Mayflower Covenant in American Myth,' *New England Quarterly*, 61:2, 233–251.

152 F. Masud-Piloto (1996) *From Welcomed Exiles to Illegal Immigrants: Cuban Migration to the U.S., 1959–1995* (Lanham, MD: Rowman and Littlefield); R. Copeland (1983) 'The Cuban Boatlift of 1980: Strategies in Federal Crisis Management,' *Annals of the American Academy of Political and Social Science*, 467, 138–150; G.D. Loescher and J. Scanlan (1981) '"Mass Asylum" and US Policy in the Caribbean,' *World Today*, 37:10, 387–395.

153 K.M. Greenhill (2002) 'Engineered Migration and the Use of Refugees as Political Weapons: A Case Study of the 1994 Cuban Balseros Crisis,' *International Migration*, 40:4, 39–74.

DOI: 10.1057/9781137502797.0009

154 H.F. Carey (2002) 'U.S. Policy in Haiti: The Failure to Help Despite the Rhetoric to Please,' *Journal of Haitian Studies*, 8:2, 86–111; J. Jefferies (2001) 'The United States and Haiti: An Exercise in Intervention,' *Caribbean Quarterly*, 47:4, 71–94.

155 See Anon. (1992) 'Haiti: The Impact of the September 1991 Coup (June 1992),' *International Journal of Refugee Law*, 4:2, 217–229; B. Frelick (1993) 'Haitian Boat Interdiction and Return: First Asylum and First Principles of Refugee Protection,' *Cornell International Law Journal*, 26:3, 675–694; A.C. Helton (1993) 'United States Government Program of Intercepting and Forcibly Returning Haitian Boat People to Haiti: Policy Implications and Prospects,' *New York Law School Journal of Human Rights*, 10:2, 325–350; M. Lennox (1993) 'Refugees, Racism, and Reparations: A Critique of United States' Haitian Immigration Policy,' *Stanford Law Review*, 45:3, 687–724; S.H. Legomsky (2006) 'The USA and the Caribbean Interdiction Program,' *International Journal of Refugee Law*, 18:3–4, 677–695.

156 H. Von Gemund (2006) 'From Somalia to Yemen: Great Dangers, Few Prospects,' *Forced Migration Review*, 27, 67–69.

157 R. Stern (2014) '"Our Refugee Policy is Generous": Reflections on the Importance of a State's Self-Image,' *Refugee Survey Quarterly*, 33:1, 25–43; C. Levy (2010) 'Refugees, Europe, Camps/State of Exception: "Into the Zone", the European Union and Extraterratorial Processing of Migrants, Refugees, and Asylum-Seekers (Theories and Practice),' ibid., 29:1, 92–119.

158 D.L. Zinn (1996) 'Adriatic Brethren or Black Sheep? Migration in Italy and the Albanian Crisis, 1991,' *European Urban and Regional Studies*, 3:3, 241–249; T. Perlmutter (1998) 'The Politics of Proximity: The Italian Response to the Albanian Crisis,' *International Migration Review*, 32:1, 203–222.

159 M. Baldwin-Edwards (2006) '"Between a Rock and a Hard Place": North Africa as a Region of Emigration, Immigration and Transit Migration,' *Review of African Political Economy*, 33:108, 311–324; S. Kneebone et al. (2006) 'A Mediterranean Solution? Chances of Success,' *International Journal of Refugee Law*, 18:3–4, 492–508; V. Moreno-Lax (2011) 'Seeking Asylum in the Mediterranean: Against a Fragmentary Reading of EU Member States' Obligations Accruing at Sea,' ibid., 23:2, 174–220.

160 C. Mainwaring (2012) 'In the Face of Revolution: The Libyan Civil War and Migration Politics in Southern Europe,' in S. Callaya et al. (eds.) *The EU and Political Change in Neighbouring Regions: Lessons for EU Interactions with the Southern Mediterranean* (Valetta: Malta University Press), 431–451; M. Hendow (2013) 'Tunisian Migrant Journeys: Human Rights Concerns for Tunisians Arriving by Sea,' *Laws*, 2:3, 187–209; S. Grant (2011) 'Recording and Identifying European Frontier Deaths,' *European Journal of Migration and Law*, 13:1, 135–156; R. Andrijasevic (2010) 'Deported: The Right to Asylum at EU's External Border of Italy and Libya,' *International*

DOI: 10.1057/9781137502797.0009

Migration, 48:1, 148–174; B. Nascimbene and A. di Pascale (2011) 'The "Arab Spring" and the Extraordinary Influx of People Who Arrived in Italy from North Africa,' *European Journal of Migration and Law*, 13:2, 341–360.

161 C. Mainwaring (2012) 'Constructing a Crisis: The Role of Immigration Detention in Malta,' *Population, Space and Place*, 18:6, 687–700; S. Klepp (2011) 'A Double Bind: Malta and the Rescue of Unwanted Migrants at Sea, a Legal Anthropological Perspective on the Humanitarian Law of the Sea,' *International Journal of Refugee Law*, 23:3, 538–557.

162 H. Van Houtum and F. Boedeltje (2009) 'Europe's Shame: Death at the Borders of Europe,' *Antipode*, 41:2, 226–230; J. Carling (2007) 'Migration Control and Migrant Fatalities at the Spanish-African Borders,' *International Migration Review*, 41:2, 316–343.

163 T. Gammeltoft-Hansen (2008) 'The Refugee, the Sovereign and the Sea: European Union Interdiction Policies,' in R. Adler-Nissen and T. Gammeltoft-Hansen (eds.) *Sovereignty Games: Instrumentalizing State Sovereignty in Europe and Beyond* (New York: Palgrave Macmillan), 171–195; J. Cobbens (2012) 'Migrants in the Mediterranean: Do's and Don'ts in Maritime Interdiction,' *Ocean Development and International Law*, 43:4, 342–370; E. Papastavridis (2010) 'Fortress Europe and FRONTEX: Within or Without International Law,' *Nordic Journal of International Law*, 79, 75–111; S. Léonard (2010) 'EU Border Security and Migration into the European Union: FRONTEX and Securitisation through Practices,' *European Security*, 19:2, 231–254; S.M. Reid-Henry (2013) 'An Incorporating Geopolitics: Frontex and the Geopolitical Rationalities of the European Border,' *Geopolitics*, 18:1, 198–224; A.N. Neal (2009) 'Securitization and Risk at the EU Border: The Origins of FRONTEX,' *Journal of Common Market Studies*, 47:2, 333–356.

164 S. Klepp (2010) 'A Contested Asylum System: The European Union between Refugee Protection and Border Control in the Mediterranean Sea,' *European Journal of Migration and Law*, 12:1, 1–22; M. Garlick (2006) 'The EU Discussions on Extraterritorial Processing: Solution or Conundrum,' *International Journal of Refugee Law*, 18:3, 601–629; A. Francis (2008) 'Bringing Protection Home: Healing the Schism between International Obligations and National Safeguards Created by Extraterritorial Processing,' ibid., 20:2, 273–313.

DOI: 10.1057/9781137502797.0009

6
Conclusion

Abstract: *The conclusion sums up the main findings and identifies various types of camps according to their primary and secondary functions and lists the functional equivalents of camps. While acknowledging that camps constitute a very widespread phenomenon, it also underlines that they are always the exception, that is, heterotopias or 'outsides inside.' In their benign forms they may constitute 'humanitarian spaces,' but they often also have much more sinister functions. The chapter also points to the need for further research.*

Keywords: camp typology; heterotopias; humanitarian space; safe havens

Møller, Bjørn. *Refugees, Prisoners and Camps: A Functional Analysis of the Phenomenon of Encampment.* Basingstoke: Palgrave Macmillan, 2015. DOI: 10.1057/9781137502797.0010.

The analysis of camps and their functional equivalents in this book has, hopefully, shown that we are faced with quite a diverse and multifaceted range of phenomena, as summarised in Table 6.1.

TABLE 6.1   *Camps: taxonomy and functions*

Functions category	Primary functions	Secondary functions	Functional substitutes	
Prisons	Punishment	Detention	Deportation	Internal Penal Colonies
		Correction	Panopticism	Religion Surveillance
Concentration Camps	Detention	Forced labour	Ghettos	
	Extermination		*Einsatzgruppen*	
	Detention (POWs)		Murder/Release	
War Camps	Training Camps	Indoctrination	The Internet	
	Separation (Combatant/Civilian)	Social Engineering	Undefended Cities	
Refugee/IDP Camps	Humanitarian Assistance	Sanctuary for combatants	Repatriation to home country Asylum in host country	

Even though neither states nor local authorities previously experienced any need for incarcerating deviants and miscreants for lengthy periods – considering that it was both easier and cheaper to either letting them go or flog, behead or hang them for the sake of public order – most countries today feel a need for prisons of various sorts. Camp-like institutions such as prisons are thus used as 'storage facilities' for those undesirables who would otherwise disturb the life of 'decent folk,' but they could presumably also serve other purposes. If these penal venues are sufficiently unpleasant, then the risk of ending up behind bars will presumably deter prospective troublemakers in general or at the very least deter first-time offenders from pursuing a career of crime. Moreover, according to progressive prison reformers such as Bentham, the constant gaze in a specially designed 'panoptic' prison might even transform deviants into respectable law-abiding citizens.

Depending on the penological ambition, however, there were also functional equivalents to incarceration such as internal or external deportation – either to penal colonies such as colonial Australia or to the distant, dark and desolate parts of Siberia where fencing was even deemed superfluous as escape was only possible by means of 'strategic cannibalism.' Just as deportation could be substituted for imprisonment,

DOI: 10.1057/9781137502797.0010

a Benthamian panoptic gaze with its assumed psychotherapeutical effects might also be achieved by other forms of observation, either by the omniscient Almighty himself (as preached by the church) or, in the modern and postmodern world, by means of Orwellian 'Big Brother' surveillance of everybody's behaviour by a wide variety of electronic means such as closed-circuit television (CCTV), both in the public space and in the privacy of their own homes, or in the new domain of cyberspace.

While camps may serve as prisons for actual or prospective criminals, they may also serve as 'antechambers of death' or even as places of slaughter as was the case of the worst Nazi concentration camps. While some of these were used as actual prisons, mainly for political opponents, others were the sites of slave labour on a gargantuan scale or even intended for working people to death. Still others were used as transit facilities for the intended victims of genocide, and a few served as veritable 'death factories,' killing at an unprecedented speed as in Auschwitz.

While most of this killing took place during a war, it did not so much serve the purpose of war as, by consuming scarce services such as those of the railways, it worked against the rationale of winning the war. However, the war itself – as wars since times immemorial have done – created a need for other kinds of camps. Some camps were intended to house former enemy combatants who were by capture, surrender or injury transformed into prisoners-of-war (POWs) endowed with rights and with an international organisation, the International Committee of the Red Cross (ICRC) serving as custodian of these rights and inspector of the POW camps. The encampment of former soldiers rendered *hors de combat* thus marked the threshold between combatants whom it was legitimate to kill and civilians protected by civilian immunity, but there were other means of making such distinctions. The mainly declaratory transformation of towns and cities into 'undefended sites' provided some protection for the residents by making attacks against them punishable as war crimes. In the same category we might also place the establishment of 'safe havens,' for example, formally (but often not successfully) protected by UN declarations and defended by 'blue helmets.'[1]

The establishment of camp-like and usually enclosed 'strategic hamlets' in the countryside served the same purpose of constituting sanctuaries for those inside the perimeter, thereby transforming everybody found outside into legitimate targets. As an added benefit, it also allowed for some social engineering inside the camps, for example, by temporarily

DOI: 10.1057/9781137502797.0010

capturing the hitherto 'uncaptured peasantry' which was viewed as an impediment to state-building – a problem which regimes had previously sought to solve via forced agricultural collectivisation, usually with catastrophic consequences.

A final type of camps are those established by presumably altruistic and unselfish humanitarians for the protection of innocent victims of persecution and violence, that is, refugee and internally displaced person (IDP) camps. Their benign nature as 'humanitarian spaces' notwithstanding,[2] even such camps are not without problems, as they require governance structures where largely unaccountable humanitarian personnel exercise power over camp inmates with few choices and reduced to humiliating roles as aid recipients and, indeed, to Agambian undignified 'bare life.'[3] In some cases refugee camps even become militarised, for example, serving as convenient sites for the recruitment of fighters or even as military base areas where de facto combatants might enjoy some protection by blending in with other camp inmates enjoying civilian immunity. Hence the temptation, to which many warring parties have indeed succumbed, to attack such militarised camps, in blatant violation of international humanitarian law, but nevertheless often with de facto impunity.

All of the above diversity raises legitimate doubts about whether we are in fact dealing with one multifaceted phenomenon or several different phenomena which just happen to be designated with the same term. What the above analyses of various types of camps and camp-like phenomena has, hopefully, shown is that there is something more to it than that, and that the various examples simply resemble in some, but not all and not necessarily the same, respects a Weberian ideal-type ('The Camp'), which is thus best understood as an analytical construct, that is, a *Gedankenbild*.

What all the camps and camp-like phenomena have in common is that they establish separations, be that between the good and the bad, decent folk and deviants, valuable matter and dirt,[4] legitimate and illegitimate targets, and sometimes even between valued and worthless lives, *bios* and *zoe*. Camps are thus 'heterotopias' in the Foucauldian sense of sites of exception or 'outsides inside,' and their proliferation –in the form of either actual camps or functional equivalents thereof – thus testifies to the need of societies, both ancient and modern, for measures to maintain (at least the illusion of) homogenity and order.[5] Exactly because such 'order' is never neutral, but inevitably benefits somebody at somebody else's expense, and because theories about order, as claimed by Robert

DOI: 10.1057/9781137502797.0010

Cox, are 'always *for* someone and *for* some purpose,'[6] there is an obvious need for critical analysis, to which end this thin monograph has, hopefully, made a modest contribution.

Notes

1　J. Hyndman (2003) 'Preventive, Palliative, or Punitive? Safe Spaces in Bosnia-Herzegovina, Somalia, and Sri Lanka,' *Journal of Refugee Studies*, 16:2, 167–185; K. Landgren (1995) 'Safety Zones and International Protection: A Dark Grey Area,' *International Journal of Refugee Law*, 7:3, 436–458, P.S. Subedi (1999) 'The Legal Competence of the International Community to Create "Safe Havens" in "Zones of Turmoil",' *Journal of Refugee Studies*, 12:1, 23–35.

2　M. Acuto (ed.) (2014) *Negotiating Relief: The Politics of Humanitarian Space* (London: Hurst) (n. 260).

3　G. Agamben (1998) *Homo Sacer: Sovereign Power and Bare Life* (Stanford, CA: Stanford University Press).

4　As in M. Douglas' (1966) definition of dirt as 'matter out of place' in *Purity and Danger: An Analysis of the Concepts of Pollution and Taboo* (London: Routledge and Kegan Paul), 35.

5　M. Foucault (2002) *The Order of Things: An Archaeology of the Human Sciences* (London: Routledge), xix; idem and J. Miskowiec (1986) 'Of Other Spaces,' *Diacritics*, 16:1 (n. 14).

6　R.W. Cox (1986) 'Social Forces, States and World Orders: Beyond International Relations Theory,' in R. Keohane (ed.) *Neorealism and Its Critics* (New York: Columbia University Press), 204–254, quote from 207.

DOI: 10.1057/9781137502797.0010

Selective Bibliography

Acuto, M. ed. (2014) *Negotiating Relief: The Politics of Humanitarian Space* (London: Hurst).

Agamben, G. (1998) *Homo Sacer: Sovereign Power and Bare Life* (Stanford, CA: Stanford University Press).

Agier, V. (2008) *On the Margins of the World: The Refugee Experience Today* (Cambridge: Polity Press).

———. (2011) *Managing the Undesirables: Refugee Camps and Humanitarian Government* (Cambridge: Polity Press).

Applebaum, A. (2004) *Gulag: A History* (London: Penguin).

Barnett, M. (2011) *Empire of Humanity: A History of Humanitarianism* (Ithaca, NY: Cornell University Press).

Betts, A. (2009) *Forced Migration and Global Politics* (Oxford: Wiley-Blackwell).

Betts, A. et al. (2012) *UNHCR: The Politics and Practice of Refugee Protection.* 2nd ed. (London: Routledge).

Caplan, J. and N. Wachsmann, eds. (2010). *Concentration Camps in Nazi Germany* (London: Routledge).

Cohen, R. and Deng, F.M. (1998). *Masses in Flight: The Global Crisis of Internal Displacement* (Washington, DC: Brookings Institution Press).

De Forges, A. (1999) *Leave None to Tell the Story: Genocide in Rwanda* (New York: Human Rights Watch).

Deng, F.M. (1993) *Protecting the Dispossessed: A Challenge for the International Community* (Washington, DC: Brookings Institution).

Feig, K.G. (1979) *Hitler's Death Camps: The Sanity of Madness* (New York: Holmes and Meier).

DOI: 10.1057/9781137502797.0011

Foucault, M. (1991) *Discipline and Punish: The Birth of the Prison* (London: Penguin).

Gutman, Y. and M. Berenbaum (1998) *Anatomy of the Auschwitz Death Camp* (Bloomington, IN: Indiana University Press).

Haddad, E. (2008) *The Refugee in International Society: Between Sovereigns* (Cambridge: Cambridge University Press).

Horst, C. (2006) *Transnational Nomads: How Somalis Cope with Refugee Life in the Dadaab Camps of Kenya* (New York: Berghahn Books).

Kiernan, B. (2008) *The Pol Pot Regime: Race, Power, and Genocide in Cambodia under the Khmer Rouge, 1975–79.* 3rd ed. (New Haven, CT: Yale University Press).

Kogon, E. (2006) *The Theory and Practice of Hell: The German Concentration Camps and the System Behind Them.* 2nd ed. (New York: Farrar, Straus and Giroux).

Lischer, S.K. (2005) *Dangerous Sanctuaries: Refugee Camps, Civil War, and the Dilemmas of Humanitarian Aid* (Ithaca, NY: Cornell University Press).

Loescher, G. et al., eds. (2008) *Protracted Refugee Situations: Political, Human Rights and Security Implications* (Tokyo: United Nations University Press).

Maguire, M. et al., eds. (2007) *The Oxford Handbook of Criminology.* 4th ed. (Oxford: Oxford University Press).

Malkki, L.H. (1995) *Purity and Exile: Violence, Memory, and National Cosmology among Hutu Refugees in Tanzania* (Chicago, IL: Chicago University Press).

Mamdani, M. (2001) *When Victims Become Killers: Colonialism, Nativism, and the Genocide in Rwanda* (Oxford: James Currey).

Marfleet, P. (2006) *Refugees in the Global Era* (Houndmills: Palgrave Macmillan).

Melvern, L. (2000) *A People Betrayed: The Role of the West in Rwanda's Genocide* (London: Zed Books).

———. (2004) *Conspiracy to Murder: The Rwandan Genocide* (London: Verso).

Michman, D. (2011) *The Emergence of Jewish Ghettos during the Holocaust* (Cambridge: Cambridge University Press).

Mogire, E. (2011) *Victims as Security Threats: Refugee Impact on Host State Security in Africa* (Farham, Surrey: Ashgate).

Morris, N. and D.J. Rothman, eds. (1998) *The Oxford History of the Prison: The Practice of Punishment in Western Society* (Oxford: Oxford University Press).

DOI: 10.1057/9781137502797.0011

Mytum, H. and G. Carr, eds. (2013) *Prisoners of War: Archaeology, Memory, and Heritage of 19th- and 20th-Century Mass Internment* (New York: Springer).

Prunier, G. (1999) *The Rwanda Crisis: History of a Genocide.* 2nd ed. (Kampala: Fountain Publishers).

Sofsky, W. (1997) *The Order of Terror: The Concentration Camp* (Princeton, NJ: Princeton University Press).

Straus, S. (2006) *The Order of Genocide: Race, Power and War in Rwanda* (Ithaca, NY: Cornell University Press).

Terry, F. (2002) *Condemned to Repeat? The Paradox of Humanitarian Action* (Ithaca, NY: Cornell University Press).

Trunk, I. (1996) *Judenrat: The Jewish Councils in Eastern Europe under Nazi Occupation.* 2nd ed. (Lincoln, NE: University of Nebraska Press)

Turner, S. (2010) *Politics of Innocence: Hutu Identity, Conflict and Camp Life* (Oxford: Berghahn Books).

Vincent, M. and B.R. Sorensen, eds. (2001) *Caught between Borders: Response Strategies of the Internally Displaced* (London: Pluto Press).

DOI: 10.1057/9781137502797.0011

Index

DOI: 10.1057/9781137502797.0012

DOI: 10.1057/9781137502797.0012

DOI: 10.1057/9781137502797.0012

Lightning Source UK Ltd.
Milton Keynes UK
UKOW02n1233220415

250117UK00003B/25/P